PARENTING
by THE BOOK™

PARENTING
by THE BOOK™

Biblical Wisdom for Raising Your Child

John Rosemond

HOWARD BOOKS
A DIVISION OF SIMON & SCHUSTER
New York   London   Toronto   Sydney

Our purpose at Howard Books is to:

- *Increase faith* in the hearts of growing Christians
- *Inspire holiness* in the lives of believers
- *Instill hope* in the hearts of struggling people everywhere

Because He's coming again!

HOWARD
BOOKS

Published by Howard Books, a division of Simon & Schuster, Inc.
1230 Avenue of the Americas, New York, NY 10020
www.howardpublishing.com

Parenting by The Book™ © 2007 John K. Rosemond

10

HOWARD colophon is a registered trademark of Simon & Schuster, Inc.

Manufactured in the United States

For information regarding special discounts for bulk purchases, please contact: Simon & Schuster Special Sales at 1-800-456-6798 or business @simonandschuster.com.

Edited by Mary McNeil
Cover design by The Designworks Group
Interior design by Jaime Putorti

Library of Congress Cataloging-in-Publication Data

Rosemond, John K., 1947–
Parenting by the book : biblical wisdom for raising your child / John Rosemond.
    p. cm.
  Summary: "Parenting book based on biblical principles with concrete suggestions on how to better raise children, developing self-respect rather than self-esteem:— Provided by publisher.
1. Parenting—Religious aspects—Christianity. 2. Child rearing—Religious aspects—Christianity. I. Title.
  BV4529.R67 2007
  248.8'45—dc22
                    2007019593

ISBN-13: 978-1-4165-4484-5
ISBN-10:   1-4165-4484-4

To Jesus Christ, who surprised me by showing up when he did, and who has since renewed everything about my life and given my work new purpose.

And to my dear mother, Emily Moore Webb,
for giving me such a great and wonderful start.
Thanks for the memories, Mom.

CONTENTS

THANK YOU!

My errors are mine alone, and any criticisms due this work are due to my own shortcomings, but for anything herein that is true, accurate, on the money, moving, and the genuine real deal, my thanks go to the following good people:

Lee Strobel, for scraping the scales off my denying eyes.

Chuck Colson and Philip Yancey, for helping me find my way to the salt mine.

Jill Rigby, for putting Denny Boultinghouse and me and Steve Laube and me together, and for being a good friend and a source of continuing inspiration.

Denny Boultinghouse, my editor-of-final-word at Howard Books and fellow blues traveler, for believing in me and this project; also for his faith, fellowship, musical selections, and wonderfully impish sense of humor, and for his patience as I felt my way into this ministry; as is the case with Willie and me, Denny's lovely wife, Philis, is obviously his better 90 percent.

John, Chrys, Linda, Susan, and everyone at Howard Books for their support through this project.

Steve Laube, my agent, for his support, encouragement, commitment to seeing that this book finds its audience, fellowship, and his faith in my ability to keep crankin' 'em out, which is my intention, God willing.

Mary McNeil, my editor, for her affirmation, her corrections, her diligence, and her sense of humor; when I found out she rode a Harley, I knew I was in good hands.

Elizabeth Stevens, my bookings manager, for her patience, good nature, and commitment to the cause; my life on the road is a whole lot saner these days.

Bob Crittenden, the Reverend John Kirtley, and Dr. Timothy Scott, for reading pages-in-progress and sharing invaluable comments and suggestions.

Glenn Stanton of Focus on the Family, for his patience and commitment to seeing that I got it right.

Dr. DuBose Ravenel, for his excellent help in getting me started on this project, and his invaluable advice along the way.

Willie, my wife and best friend, for her support during the writing of this book, which took lots of time away from our relationship, which she graciously gave, and for her steadfast love of this sinner man; you rock, and you are the rock, my love.

INTRODUCTION

The Journey So Far

When the foundations are being destroyed,
what can the righteous do?
—Psalm 11:3

Several years ago, a young mother told me that she rejected "my" philosophy of parenting. After an exhaustive search of contemporary parenting literature, she had decided that "attachment parenting" suited her best. Suited her? This was postmodernity (the mind-set that objective truth does not exist and everything is relative) talking. As The Rolling Stones, in what may be the most postmodern of lyrics, put it, "I'm free to do what I want, any old time." As I pointed out to this mother, the matter of how a child should be raised is not about the parent; it's about the child. Furthermore, whereas there may be more than one way to skin the proverbial cat, there is but one correct way to raise a child. (If you think I'm making this statement presumptuously, I encourage you to read on.) But in fairness, the mental health community has been anything but of one voice where child rearing is concerned, and each of the competing voices in the cacophony of psychobabble has claimed and claims superiority. Choosing to listen to only one may be the only way to maintain one's sanity.

One might ask what's different about John Rosemond's way of raising children, to which the answer is that John Rosemond's way does not exist. The way described in these pages is straight from the Bible. I am a messenger, and a somewhat paradoxical one at that.

I possess a license to practice psychology, issued by the North Carolina Psychology Board. In that sense, I am a psychologist. But unlike most of those who hold such licenses, I have major problems with the direction my once noble profession has taken since the late 1960s, when the American Psychological Association was hijacked by secular progressives who were focused more on advancing humanist ideology than advancing the human condition.

A number of years ago, I came to the realization that for all of its pretenses to scientific objectivity, post-1960s psychology is a secular religion that one believes in by faith. I had been slowly losing that false faith since the early 1980s, but I lost the last vestige seven years ago, when I submitted my life to Jesus Christ.

I am absolutely convinced that modern psychology has done more harm than good to the American family. Not "family," mind you, the various alternatives of which the American Psychological Association has enthusiastically affirmed, even actively promoted, but family, as in heterosexual parents and children related by birth or adoption. The reason child rearing—once a fairly straightforward, matter-of-fact affair—has become so difficult, so emotionally taxing, so beset with problems, is that instead of going to their elders for child-rearing advice, American parents have been listening to mental health professionals tell them how to raise children for more than a generation. With rare but notable exception—Dr. James Dobson, Dr. Kevin Leman, and a handful of others—the advice has been bad. Since the mid-1960s, when nouveau "parenting" began to displace traditional Biblically based child rearing, the mental health of America's kids has been in a downward spiral, the end of which has yet to come into view. But children are not the only ones who have suffered the toxins of professional advice. The raising of a child, once a fairly straightforward, commonsense affair, has become the single most stressful thing a woman will do in her lifetime. The mothers I talk to around the United States concur when I suggest that raising a child is more anxiety-ridden than managing a large staff of people at a major corporation. That's not the way God planned it, but then God's way is not modern psychology's way, either.

Beginning with Sigmund Freud (1856–1939), the father of modern psychology, mental health professionals have cut one idea after another out of whole cloth. It surprises people when I tell them that none of Freud's theories has been verified; in fact, most of them have been discredited. After all, he made them up. He was convinced he had the last word on human reality—that he possessed unique powers of insight into the workings of the mind, any thought he had was true, and everyone else needed to know what his great mind was producing. It was inconceivable to Freud that he was wrong about anything. Over the years, psychological theories have come, and psychological theories have gone. The theories have been different, but it's always been the same old, same old, come-and-go. Since Freud, the history of psychology has been the history of one failed diagnosis, theory, and therapy after another: multiple personality disorder, recovered memory therapy, psychoanalytic theory and therapy, Gestalt therapy, play therapy, and so on and so on. Freud also began moving the profession toward atheism. He thought religion was a neurosis, and there are many in the profession today who feel similarly. I would venture that clinical psychologists, as a group, have less regard for God than is the case with any other single group of professionals. Again, that's not true of *all* psychologists, but it's certainly characteristic of the mainstream, of which John Rosemond, James Dobson, and Kevin Leman are not members.

One of my disagreements with my profession has to do with the idea that attending graduate school makes one competent to counsel people who are having personal or relationship trouble in their lives. Competent counseling comes from the Holy Spirit, and the Holy Spirit has no preference for PhDs. My barber, a believer, gives about the best counsel I've ever gotten from anyone. Whenever I'm grappling with a personal issue, I schedule a haircut.

I am a psychologist with a Christian perspective. That's a difficult balancing act because the worldview of Christianity and the worldview of contemporary, post-1960s, secular psychology are poles apart.

Psychology holds that the individual is fundamentally good. Christianity holds that human beings, whereas created in the image of God, corrupted all of creation by rebelling against him.

Psychology's central doctrine is one of nonresponsibility—fundamentally, the individual is the product of his upbringing; therefore, his vices are reflections of psychic conflicts engendered by his parents' inadequacies (i.e., the individual, fundamentally good, is messed up by his parents, who were messed up by their parents, and so on). According to psychology, a person is a chronic liar because during his childhood he was made to feel responsible for protecting certain family secrets, such as his father's alcoholism and his mother's tryst with the next-door neighbor. He can't hold a job because his father was threatened by his achievements, so to achieve is to betray his father. He has three failed marriages because he secretly believes that, like his mother, no woman can be trusted. And so on. Christianity holds that we are solely and fully responsible for our sinful behavior and that only by accepting that responsibility can we receive forgiveness.

Psychology holds that a person can be "saved" through the process of therapy as mediated by another human being, that coming to grips with the corruption suffered at the hands of one's parents will set one free. Christianity holds that salvation is attained only through faith in Jesus Christ, that he is the Truth, and that only his truth can set one free.

So, to answer the above question, I am not a Christian psychologist. I am a Christian who holds a license to practice psychology. I believe Jesus Christ is the one and only Wonderful Counselor. It is only through him that a broken person can be made truly whole again.

> *For to us a child is born, to us a son is given. . . . And he will be called Wonderful Counselor, Mighty God, Everlasting Father, Prince of Peace.*
>
> *—ISAIAH 9:6*

I began to realize that psychology was a secular religion when my licensing board accused me of professional misconduct in the early 1990s. The misconduct involved writing a newspaper column in which I said that an eighteen-month-old child who was sexually abused on one occasion by a non–family member was "not likely to remember the event." Psychologists, clinical social workers, and marriage and family therapists all over the United States went ballistic.

At the time, one of the biggest income streams in the mental health professions was coming from "recovered memory therapy," which rested on the nonempirical notion that in a proper therapeutic environment, a person could recover memories of traumatic events that occurred even during early infancy. I was accused of violating professional ethics. In fact, I had simply pointed out that the emperor had no clothes.

During the inquisition to which I was subjected, I became acutely aware that my profession is an ideology. As such, its practitioners care little for truth. If objective research findings contradict the prevailing clinical fad, the findings are ignored, even ridiculed. It did not matter, for example, that memory research verified my position: Reliable, long-term memories do not form before the third birthday, approximately, and this rule applies to traumatic events as well as to everyday events. I had threatened the house of cards that clinical psychology had built; therefore, I had to go. In the end, my lawyers prevailed, and when it was all over, I realized that the ordeal had been a blessing in disguise. It had clarified for me that my profession was a house built on sand, and shifting sand at that. The truth began to set me free.

I still had another hurdle to clear, however. At the time, I was a cultural Christian. I went to church, I served on my church's governing board and various church committees, and I gave the church money. But all of this was a sham. I was doing nothing more than putting on a good face, a face that allowed me to avoid confronting my sinfulness, my need for forgiveness, my need for an authentic relationship with God through his Son. Even my pastor at the time told me that believing in the virgin birth, the incarnation, and the resurrection were not essential to being a good Christian. I was free to believe what I wanted, he said; what really counted was the kind of person I was, how many good deeds I performed. I took this freedom to the limit. I devoured books about the "historical Jesus"—another way of hiding, substituting intellectual curiosity for relationship.

When my sister Ann and brother-in-law Michael tried to share the Lord with me, I maintained that there were too many contradictions in the Gospels for the story to be true, and I proceeded to enumerate some of them. They patiently listened and pointed out that the mere fact four people tell the same story in slightly different ways does not discredit the story. I countered that if the story of Jesus was the truth, as they claimed, which story was the truth? How could someone possibly claim, with a straight face, that the truth came in four different forms? Exasperated, my brother-in-law told me that I was "too logical." I replied that God had given us minds with which to think logically, and if I was ever going to accept Jesus as my Lord and Savior, it was going to have to be courtesy of some logical process.

Several years later, that very thing occurred in the form of a book by Lee Strobel: *The Case for Christ*. Strobel had been an atheist when he decided to apply his training in investigative journalism to an in-depth study of the Gospels. Much to his own amazement, instead of being confirmed in his nonbelief, Strobel eventually admitted that he could not deny the validity of what Matthew, Mark, Luke, and John reported. Logic brought him to a place where he felt he had no choice but to admit and submit. Strobel had done my intellectual work for me. Upon finishing *The Case for Christ,* I admitted, and I submitted.

At this point, I'm going to ask the reader to bear with me while I backtrack a bit. During the ten years before my epiphany, I had enjoyed a reputation as one of America's premier parenting experts. After all, I was a best-selling author of eight parenting books as well as a weekly syndicated newspaper column and the busiest public speaker in my field to boot. Every so often, a pastor would approach me at a speaking engagement and say that whether I knew it or not, everything I was saying was consistent with biblical teachings concerning children and parental responsibilities. I'd listen politely and respond diplomatically, all the while looking for the nearest escape route. Sincere believers in Christ Jesus made me very nervous.

One day, somewhere in America, a minister asked me, "Have you been born again, John?"

I was stopped dead in my intellectual tracks by the simplicity, the directness, of the question. I felt trapped, suddenly in danger of being exposed as the fake I was. "I don't know," I answered.

"Then you haven't been," he said. "But someday you will be. God is preparing you, John, whether you realize it or not." With that, having completed his assignment, he politely excused himself.

He was right. I accepted Jesus as my Lord and Savior in my early fifties. That beginning in Christ was the beginning of the end of John K. Rosemond, MS, noted family psychologist. I began reading Scripture with no purpose in mind other than to strengthen my relationship with the Lord, the Word made flesh, and to nourish my new, reborn self. As I read, the fact that God has embedded in Scripture a blueprint for the raising of his children became increasingly clear. I began having one "Whoa!" experience after another as the blueprint slowly unrolled before my eyes. Some of the blueprint's details are obvious, such as Proverbs 22:6: "Train a child in the way he should go, and when he is old he will not turn from it." And some are not so obvious, such as Jesus's instruction to his disciples in Matthew 5:37: "Simply let your 'Yes' be 'Yes,' and your 'No,' 'No.'" What an elegantly simple and straightforward way of expressing the foundation of proper discipline!

One of the many miracles of Scripture revealed itself to me: It is all things to all people in every time. To find, one must simply seek. If one opens the Bible seeking marital guidance, the Bible will become, in his or her hands, a manual on how to properly conduct oneself within marriage. If one opens the Bible seeking advice on how to conduct oneself in a business relationship, the Bible will become a guide to business ethics. For a parent seeking guidance in child-rearing matters, the Bible will become a parenting manual. And so on. I was amazed, to say the least.

Every Christian is a minister. Each Christian's ministry is unique. You don't choose it for yourself; it's chosen for you. As I listened to God with an open heart, I realized that he had given me an assignment—this ministry to America's families that I call *Parenting by The Book*.

People sometimes tell me that they like my ideas. I am quick to point out that what they think are my ideas are not my own, that I am a messenger, nothing more. With my tongue planted firmly in my cheek, I call myself the Great Parenting Plagiarist because I have never had an original idea concerning the raising of children (or anything else, most likely) in my life. Even when I thought I was coming up with original ideas, I was not. I was simply being prepared. My eyes were being slowly opened.

Writing this book is an act of submission to God's will. All I can do is pray that the words of my mouth (as I put them on paper) and the meditation of my heart are pleasing in his sight, for he is my Rock and my Redeemer.

I also pray that reading this book will be a blessing to you and your family, that the message contained herein will strengthen your marriage and both strengthen and "straighten" your efforts to raise responsible and compassionate citizens.

May the Lord be with you always.

John Rosemond
Gastonia, North Carolina
December 2006

PART ONE

The Great Deception

In the 1960s, secular progressives stormed the ramparts of American culture. They took sledgehammers to anything and everything traditional and erected the false gods of their new religions, the most insidious of which has been therapeutic psychology. The new psychology, unleashed from the restraints of objectivity, was programmed to aid in the destruction of the intact nuclear family, and a good job it has done. Mental health professionals attacked the legitimacy of the traditional marriage and demonized traditional child rearing, both of which are founded on biblical principles. Parenting according to Dr. So-and-So replaced parenting according to God's design, and it's been a downhill ride ever since.

CHAPTER ONE

The Walls Come Crumblin' Down

Blessed is the man who makes the LORD his trust.
—PSALM 40:4

O ur journey begins in 2002, in Lafayette, Louisiana. I'm in the lobby of an auditorium in which I'm about to speak, chatting with several parents. One of the women suddenly says, "I'm absolutely convinced, John, that my husband and I have experienced more problems in four years with two children than my parents had with all ten of us the entire time."

That mother's statement reflects the difficulties inherent in today's child-rearing philosophy and practice. Further, it echoes not just the experience of one set of parents in Lafayette, but the experience of many if not most parents in the United States. Whether you grew up in a large or small family, you are almost certainly experiencing more child-rearing difficulties than did your parents—a lot more. When compared to your grandparents' child-rearing experience, there is no doubt about it. Your grandparents had problems with their children—all parents do—but compared to the problems you are having, their parenting experience was a cakewalk.

Men and women who accomplished most of their child rearing before 1960—people who are now in their seventies, eighties, and nineties—tell me that whereas they dealt with the occasional problem, the raising of children per se was not especially difficult. As one ninety-year-old woman who raised five children during the forties and fifties once told me, "It was just something you did." She was by no means diminishing the responsibility. She made it clear that raising children was the most important job anyone ever undertook. She was simply putting it in its proper perspective: Raising children was but one of *many* responsibilities she had assumed as an adult, and she had been determined to execute each and every one of them to the best of her ability. These included responsibilities as a daughter, sister, friend, wife, employee (she had worked as a secretary for a number of years), member of various women's clubs and civic organizations, and member of her church. Because she did not overidentify with the role of mother, she was not overfocused on her kids. Therefore, raising children did not consume, exasperate, and exhaust her. She was able to discharge her responsibilities to her children, including their discipline, in a calm, collected, confident fashion. That hardly describes the day-to-day experience of today's oft-consumed, oft-exasperated, and oft-exhausted parents, and mothers especially.

THE TIMES, THEY ARE A-CHANGIN'

"But, John!" someone might exclaim. "Times have changed!"

That cliché really explains nothing. "Times" have always changed, but until recently, the raising of children did not change from generation to generation. As technology, demographics, and economic conditions changed, the general approach to child rearing remained pretty much the same. My grandparents, for example, were born in the 1890s. During the first thirty years of their lives, they witnessed and experienced more change—in every conceivable fashion—than has occurred in the last thirty years (since 1977). Yet child rearing did not change during that time. My parents were born around 1920. Consider the dramatic changes that took place during the first thirty years of their lives, from 1920 to 1950: a worldwide depression that lasted more than a decade, a global war that lasted for five years, the development and use of nuclear weapons, the start of the Cold War and the national insecurity that resulted, the invention of television, and the ubiquity of the automobile. These events transformed not only America, but the world. No one born after 1950 has experienced such profound cultural transformation. Yet from 1920 to 1950, child rearing in America did not change in any appreciable way. My grandparents raised my parents in accord with the same child-rearing principles that had guided my great-grandparents, and they employed pretty much the same methods. My point: The mere fact that "times" change neither means nor requires change in every single thing.

Once upon a time, people understood that in changing times, certain things should not change; that there must always be certain constants in culture. A short list of those changeless things includes consensus concerning morality, the need for adults to be contributing members of society, and constants regarding how the family should function, including how children should be brought up. Once upon a time, people understood that change would deteriorate into chaos unless change was organized around unchanging "still points" in the culture, and child rearing was one of those points. In fact, there is no evidence that in the Judeo-Christian world the fundamental principles governing child rearing had appreciably changed since its founding by Abraham and Sarah. For thousands of years, the child-rearing "baton" was handed down, intact, from generation to generation. Children *honored* their parents by growing up and raising their children the same way their parents had raised them, and let there be no doubt: the "way" in question was based on biblical principles.[1]

> *Honor your father and your mother, so that you may live long in the land the LORD your God is giving you.*
> —EXODUS 20:12

Progress constantly infuses culture with new energy, but in the fifth commandment God promises a stable, secure society to people who adhere to fundamental family traditions. But that understanding went by the boards in the 1960s, the single most deconstructive decade in the history of the United States of America.

Something New under the Sun

During the 1960s, the United States underwent a culture-wide paradigm shift that had profound effect on all of our institutions, including the family. Before the sixties, we were a culture informed by and defined by tradition. Progress took place in nearly every generation, but most people continued to embrace traditional values and live their lives according to traditional form. When young people reached adulthood, developed occupations, married, and had children, they adopted their parents' values and consciously sought to emulate their parents' examples. (Exceptions to any general rule can always be found, but this was certainly a general rule.) There had been a minor challenge to this constancy after World War I, but it came completely undone in the 1960s. America entered the 1960s one culture and emerged from that tumultuous decade a different culture altogether, in every respect. By 1970, we were no longer a culture informed and defined by tradition, but a culture informed and defined by a relatively new electronic medium—television—a medium that had decided to promote a radical, progressive agenda.

During television's infancy in the 1950s, television programs, without exception, reflected traditional American values. Perhaps you're old enough to remember (or perhaps you've seen the reruns) *I Love Lucy, The Donna Reed Show, Father Knows Best, Leave It to Beaver, Lassie, Walt Disney Presents,* and variety shows like *The Ed Sullivan Show.*

In the 1960s, however, the now-adolescent television industry began to take on a rebellious, activist character. Its movers and shakers became determined to use the influence of television to reshape America consistent with the vision of the emerging neoliberal, secular elite. And they succeeded.

By 1970, the consensus that had previously existed concerning values, right versus wrong, and morality had begun to unravel. All of the "still points" that had previously stabilized America had been undermined and were beginning to topple.

By the mid-1970s, the United States had become a full-fledged "progressive" culture. Progressivism holds that just as most new technologies (such as computers) are better than old technologies (typewriters), new *ideas* are better than old ideas. For the most part, the progressive mind-set rejects tradition. It refuses to recognize that there is, in truth, "nothing new under the sun," as a wise man wrote thousands of years ago: "What has been will be again, what has been done will be done again; there is nothing new under the sun" (Ecclesiastes 1:9).

Many in my generation—the Baby Boomers—became seduced by the new utopian progressivism. We (as a much younger man, I identified with this movement) deluded ourselves into thinking that we had been anointed by some secular divinity to usher out everything old and ring in a Brave New World. We decided that traditional values and forms had to go—that our parents' values were most definitely *not* going to be our values, and their ways of doing things were most definitely *not* going to be our ways. One of the old ways in question was traditional child rearing.

Grandma's Homespun Wisdom

Before the 1960s, when parents had problems with their children, they did not seek advice from people with capital letters after their names. Rather, they sought the counsel of elders in their extended families, churches, and communities. "Grandma"—the generic term I use to refer to the elders in question—was the universally recognized child-rearing expert. Grandma gave child-rearing advice based on the life she had led. Furthermore, the advice she gave concerning any given parenting problem was the same advice her mother would have given her under similar circumstances, and the same advice her grandmother would have given her mother, and so on down the generations.

After the 1960s, parents were no longer going to Grandma for child-rearing advice. Instead, they were seeking counsel from people in the mental health professions—people who dispensed advice based not on lives they had led, but rather on books they had read.

Understanding what Grandma was talking about did not require a college degree. She did not say things like, "In talking with you, I get the distinct impression that you are still trying to resolve childhood issues of your own, and I think we should give some time to exploring those issues and discovering how they relate to the problems you are currently having with your child." That's how people with capital letters after their names talk.

Grandma talked like this: "You know, it occurs to me that your uncle Charlie, when he was about Billy's age, did something similar to what Billy has done. Here's how I handled it. . . . You've no doubt noticed that Charlie is working for the bank today, not robbing banks. Maybe you'd like to consider going home and doing with Billy what I did with Charlie."

Young parents left their "therapy sessions" with Grandma feeling empowered and reassured, and with a clear sense of what to do. I was in private practice from 1980 to 1990. One of the sobering things that slowly dawned on me during those ten years was that parents were not always leaving their first appointments with me feeling empowered and reassured, and with a clear sense of what to do. Instead, they were sometimes leaving feeling like miserable failures because, instead of dealing with them as Grandma would have, I was doing so from behind the mask of my impressive credentials. Instead of presenting myself as simply a not-so-remarkable person who had gained some measure of wisdom as a result of my own experiences while raising children, I was presenting myself as a high and mighty, all-knowing, all-seeing psychologist. That realization eventually helped me realize I could be much more helpful to parents outside the office than if I stayed within the protection of its four diploma-ridden walls.

DESTROYING THE FOUNDATIONS

One of the changes that took place in the 1960s concerned America's attitude toward authority. Before that deconstructive decade, Americans generally respected traditional authority. A person might not have agreed with a certain politician, for example, but he still respected him. He had, after all, been duly elected, and that was that. By 1970, a cynicism and general disrespect had developed toward all forms of traditional authority, of which there are five: political, military, institutional, church, and family.

In the late sixties and early seventies, the secular, educational, and media elites began to demonize political authority, the military, institutional authority (especially within corporations), religion (especially Christianity), and the two cornerstones of the traditional family: the traditional marriage and traditional child rearing. Mind you, all of those authority traditions derived their legitimacy from the Bible. In effect, this was an assault on the very Judeo-Christian principles upon which Western civilization was built.

The attack on the traditional family was especially vicious. Psychologists and other mental health professionals allied with neofeminists to characterize the traditional family as the primary institution through which the so-called "patriarchy" exerted its domination of women and manipulation of children. This, they believed, ensured that girls would grow up willing to be dominated by men who had been trained as boys to disrespect and dominate females. Feminists equated traditional marriage with slavery and promoted "open" marriages in which neither party was obligated to be faithful. Feminists and the increasingly female-dominated mental health elite joined with the media to demonize men as natural aggressors. The 1950s father who might have worked two jobs was characterized not as responsible, wanting the best for his family, but as "remote," a guy who really cared little about either his wife or his kids, a guy who in fact used his money and physical superiority to keep them in line. Finally, mental health professionals such as psychologist Thomas Gordon, author of *Parent Effectiveness Training* (Wyden, 1970), the best-selling parenting book of the era, claimed that traditional child rearing suffocated the "natural child" and produced instead a child who was destined to become nothing more than a mindless cog in the evil capitalist machine. In one of his books, Gordon actually claimed that the traditional exercise of parental authority was a moving force behind war![2] Such was the progressive, deconstructionist hysteria on which all too many baby boomers, including a much younger John Rosemond, became intoxicated.

The Doctor Is In

During the 1960s, the television industry began to identify psychologists and other mental health professionals as the only legitimate purveyors of sound child-rearing advice. This trend had its beginnings not, as many think, with Dr. Benjamin Spock (a pediatrician), but with the elevation of psychologist Dr. Joyce Brothers to the status of a cultural icon. After winning *The $64,000 Question* (the 1950s–60s equivalent of *Who Wants to Be a Millionaire?*) in 1955, Brothers became a regular talking head on all manner of television programs. She even had her own show for a time. The networks held her up as an expert on anything and everything concerning human behavior and relationships, including how to raise children properly, and the American public listened credulously to anything and everything she had to say.

Psychologists and other mental health professionals rushed to hitch a ride on Brothers's coattails. Gordon's Parent Effectiveness Training (P.E.T.) seminars trained thousands of psychologists, family counselors, and clinical social workers in his ideas and methods. In turn, this horde of true believers shared Gordon's utopian child-rearing vision with millions of gullible American parents. One of Gordon's most devoted disciples, Dorothy Briggs, wrote the best-seller *Your Child's Self-Esteem* (Doubleday, 1970), in which she advanced the notion of the democratic family—a family in which parents and children related to one another as equals. In *YCSE*, Briggs asserted, "Democracy in government has little meaning to a child unless he feels the daily benefits of it at home."[3] She was apparently ignorant of the fact that the Founding Fathers did not grow up in democratic families yet seemed to have an exceptional grasp of democratic principles. But logic did not drive this paradigm shift; hysteria and hyperbole did.

Along about this same time, child rearing became "parenting," a new word referring to a new way of going about it. The new way transformed the parent-centered family into the child-centered family. The new way substituted high self-esteem (individualism) for respect for others (good citizenship). Parents who subscribe to the new way are not supposed to simply tell their children what to do; they are to reason with them and reward them when they "cooperate" (being de facto peers, children of enlightened parents do not simply obey).

The new way would be most satisfying to Karl Marx, who said that in order for socialism to succeed, the traditional family had to go. In that regard, there is no doubt that family psychology took on a socialist bent in the 1960s. In the 1970s I did postgraduate course work in family therapy and ultimately came to the conclusion that the real intent was to put parent and child on equal footing, to destroy the authority of parents. The authority that would step into the vacuum was the authority of the therapist, who usually sided with the kids in family disputes. The more alarming problem, however, was that I saw one set of parents after another acquiesce to this insidious kidnapping.

The new way involved not just a change in outward appearance and practice, but also a change in basic assumptions concerning the child and parental responsibilities. The traditional point of view holds that children are fundamentally bad and in need of rehabilitation; the nouveau point of view holds that children are fundamentally good. Supposedly, children no longer do bad things intentionally; they just make errors in judgment. The term most often used today is "bad choices"—mistakes, in effect, as if a child's rebellious misbehavior is no more egregious than choosing the wrong answer on a television quiz show. Because malevolent motive is absent, punishment is not warranted. Besides, punishment damages self-esteem, or so the new parenting elite warns.

So instead of punishing children when they misbehave, new parents administer what I call "therapeutic discipline" or "yada-yada discipline." That is, they talk to their children, taking care not to hurt their feelings. If repeated sessions of therapeutic yada-yada do not cause a child to start making "good choices," he is assumed to be in the grip of an "issue," a psychological conundrum from which he cannot extricate himself. His maladaptive behavior is a desperate way of drawing attention to his psychological plight and calling for help. So, whereas the old way enforced responsibility on the child for his behavior, the new way neatly absolves him of that responsibility. The misbehaving child, once a perpetrator, has become a victim, in need of therapy or drugs or both.

The Serpent's Babble

I am a member of the last generation of American children to be raised the old way—according to traditional, biblical form—and a member of the first generation of American parents to raise their children the new way, according to psychobabble. Along with others of my generation, I possess a firsthand appreciation for both the old and the new. I know that whereas child rearing wasn't perfect before the 1960s, it worked for the ultimate good of the child, the marriage, the family, the school, the community, and the culture. I also know that the new way— what I call "Postmodern Psychological Parenting"—has never worked, is not working, and never will work, no matter how diligently anyone works at it. Why?

For one thing, it makes no sense. It's composed of babble: clever, seductive babble, but babble nonetheless. But more important, it is not in harmony with God's master blueprint, which he has bequeathed us in the form of his Word, the Bible. That's why it makes no sense. It is founded not on truth, but on falsehood.

The serpent manifests itself in a different form in every generation, but its goal is always the same: to persuade God's children that God does not have their best interests at heart, that he is only trying to keep them in a state of ignorant servility, and to persuade them to turn away from him. Ultimately, Postmodern Psychological Parenting is a particularly clever manifestation of the serpent's continuing effort to undermine trust in God's authority.

Now the serpent was more crafty than any of the wild animals the LORD God had made. He said to the woman, "Did God really say, 'You must not eat from any tree in the garden'? . . . God knows that when you eat of it your eyes will be opened, and you will be like God, knowing good and evil."

—GENESIS 3:1, 5

THE BIG BLUEPRINT

God created the universe and all that is within it. The Bible tells me so, but my faith in the truthfulness of the Word is shored up by a number of relatively recent discoveries in physics, math, astronomy, and chemistry that have confirmed that the universe had a definite beginning. Before this beginning, known as the Big Bang, there was neither space nor time. There was nothing. A distinct beginning out of nothing, ex nihilo, requires the supernatural. The Big Bang means the universe had a cause, and Creation requires a Creator. It's as simple and undeniable as that.

God designed the universe such that it would support a complexity of life on one planet, and one planet only—our very own Earth.[4] The fact that all of Creation seems specifically designed with the single purpose of supporting a complexity of life on Earth means that God's act of creation was not a "throw of the dice." He was not acting out of curiosity, throwing the building blocks of the universe out there just to see how they would combine and what kind of universe would result. Rather, it is obvious that he created with intent, that he had a very specific plan, an ultimate purpose. What?

God's ultimate purpose was to provide a home for his most special creation—humankind—with whom he desired, and continues to desire, a special relationship. He endowed us and only us with the ability to know him because he wants to be known.

God has given us a big blueprint for living creative, productive, fulfilling lives and experiencing fulfilling relationships with one another and with him. This blueprint is clearly set forth in his revelation, known as the Old and New Testaments of the Bible—the Word.

The big blueprint of the Bible incorporates a number of smaller blueprints for every aspect of living, including marriage (a permanent, faithful relationship between a man and a woman), conducting business (all parties are to profit equally, albeit differently), forming and living in healthy societies (laws must be obeyed; legitimate authority and the rights of one's "neighbors" must be respected), and the rearing of children (proper discipline is as critical to proper child rearing as is love; the education of children is the responsibility of parents).

Free to Win, Free to Lose

Because God created us in his image, we possess free will. This freedom includes the freedom to choose whether we obey God, whether we live our lives in accord with his blueprints for living. Choices result in consequences. The ultimate (but not necessarily immediate) consequence of obeying God is good. The ultimate (but not necessarily immediate) consequence of disobeying God is the opposite of good. Said another way, we obey God to our credit and disobey him at our peril. Some people are uncomfortable with the notion of a righteous God who punishes wrongdoers by allowing them to experience emotional and/or physical pain; therefore, they deny the existence of God or create an alternative god in their *own* image. Their denial does not alter the fact that a loving parent does not allow a child to disobey without consequence. (As we will see, the notion of a one-dimensional god that does not punish is consistent with one of the tenets of postmodern psychology: to wit, that punishment is psychologically damaging to a child, and that loving parents, therefore, do not punish misbehavior.)

The risks of attempting to raise a child without regard for God's blueprint for child rearing, as clearly set forth in his Big Blueprint, include a child who is ill-behaved, disrespectful, destructive and self-destructive, irresponsible, inattentive, careless, aggressive, self-centered, deceitful, and so on. The risks to the child's parents include chronic frustration, stress, anxiety, anger, resentment, conflict, and guilt.

The sad, tragic fact is that most American parents, even (dare I say it?) most parents who would identify themselves as faithful believers in God and his only Son Jesus Christ, have deviated from God's child-rearing blueprint in the rearing of their children. This alone is sufficient to explain why child rearing has become the single most stressful, frustrating, anxiety- and guilt-ridden thing American adults—and especially *female* adults—will ever do. This alone is sufficient to explain why a mother in Lafayette told me that she and her husband had experienced more problems with two children in four years than had her parents during the raising of ten children.

Nothing but the Truth

This is a fact: *If you depart from God's plan in any area of your life, you will experience more (and more serious) problems than you would have encountered otherwise.* Oftentimes, those problems will seem never-ending, as if there is no light at the end of the tunnel. America has departed from God's blueprint for child rearing. That explains it all.

This is also a fact: *If you adhere to God's plan in your life, you will still experience sadness, pain, frustration, and heartache (since the Fall, there is no escaping this tribulation), but you will endure and you will eventually come out on top.* That's God's promise to us. Any parent who so chooses can realign his or her child rearing with God's plan and begin to experience success.

That's the purpose of this book. My intent is to help parents understand and properly align themselves with God's blueprint for child rearing. I can promise you this: Unlike the attempt to conform one's parenting to the many intricate and confusing dos and don'ts of Postmodern Psychological Parenting, this alignment will not strain the brain or cause doubt, anxiety, and guilt. I can make this promise with authority because of two simple truths:

1. God makes nothing complicated.

2. Conforming to God's plan in any area of life will bring relief from troubles, cares, and woes.

Come to me, all you who are weary and burdened, and I will give you rest.

—*MATTHEW 11:28*

So, with that in mind, what say we take a walk with Grandma and her Bible?

Questions for Group Discussion or Personal Reflection

1. In what specific ways does "honoring your mother and father" stabilize and sustain culture? How has the general dishonoring of the traditional family contributed to the unraveling and weakening of American culture? What are some signs that the ability to "live long in the land" is currently tenuous? How has the weakening of the traditional family contributed to a general weakening of our collective ability to respond adequately to forces that threaten America and, by extension, all of Western civilization?

2. Have you subscribed, however unwittingly, to the tenets of Postmodern Psychological Parenting? If so, what has influenced you to move in that direction?

3. Do you parent from the head or from the heart and the "gut"? In other words, do you tend to think a lot, to intellectualize about child-rearing issues or do you rely on what is called "common sense"? How does thinking a lot prevent a parent from getting in touch with common sense?

4. Like those parents in Lafayette, Louisiana, do you think you are having more problems raising your children than your parents had in raising you and your siblings? If so, what was different about your parents' approach when compared with yours?

CHAPTER TWO

Postmodern Psychological Parenting

See to it that no one takes you captive through hollow
and deceptive philosophy, which depends on human
tradition and the basic principles of this world rather
than on Christ.

—COLOSSIANS 2:8

By the mid-1970s, Grandma's common sense had been all
but drowned out by the shouts of people with capital letters after their names, who claimed that not only did Grandma
not really know what she was talking about (she hadn't gone to
college, after all), but she also had been dispensing advice that
was bad for the psychological health of children. America's parents were now in thrall to Postmodern Psychological Parenting,
an anomalous hybrid of three historically antagonistic schools
of psychological thought: Freudian, humanist, and behavioral.

- From Sigmund Freud, the father of modern psychology, comes the principle of *psychological determin-*

ism—the notion that human behavior is shaped by early childhood experiences; for example, that negative toilet training experiences can cause later personality problems.

- The humanist contribution consists of two propositions: (1) Children are fundamentally good, and (2) high self-esteem is a desirable attribute.

- Finally, the behavioral school has contributed the idea that behavior modification works as well on human beings as it does on rats and dogs.

As we will see, all three of these philosophies are bogus. They are not only antithetical to a biblical view of human nature but also contradicted by both common sense and social science research. Unfortunately, they have become so embedded in collective thought that most people take them for granted, which is why they are causing so much trouble.

FREUD BITES THE DUST

Most people would be surprised to learn that not one of Freud's ideas has survived the test of scientific scrutiny. The Oedipal complex is a fiction. Penis envy is a fiction. Oral, anal, and genital fixations are fictions. Repressed memories are a fiction. It turns out Freud made it all up. He was convinced, however, that his insights into human nature were the product of genius; therefore, he felt obliged to share them with the world. Psychological historian Hans Eysenck accurately called Freud a "genius not of science but of propaganda" whose place is not, as Freud himself humbly claimed, with Copernicus and Darwin (who had enough humility to admit that history might well prove him wrong), but with Hans Christian Andersen, the Brothers Grimm, and other tellers of fairy tales. A more recent article in *Newsweek* magazine called him "modern history's most debunked doctor."[1]

The Doctor Has No Clothes

Most significant to our purpose is the fact that Freud's claim of a cause-effect connection between early childhood experiences and maladaptive adult behavior patterns or personality kinks has never been verified. To take a popular example, the notion that premature or highly punitive toilet training can cause a so-called anal fixation that will eventually develop into obsessive-compulsiveness has not been confirmed. In fact, it's impossible to confirm. Who could accurately report on their toilet training experience? This is myth, pure and simple, as are all the supposed cause-effect connections between early parenting and adult personality.

Most people, however, believe in psychological determinism because it's the basis of much psychological therapy. If you seek professional help concerning a personal problem, the likelihood is that the therapist will engage in what I call "psychological archeology"—he will begin asking you about your childhood, and your parents in particular, in an attempt to establish a connection between then and now. And he will eventually tell you, for example, that you have difficulty making commitments because your parents put you in the middle of their messy divorce. The truth, however, is that a therapist who is seeking such a connection will most assuredly find one. He's convinced that such a connection exists before he begins his inquiry. He seeks, and he finds.

In your eyes (*you* being a typical client), his discovery testifies to his amazing powers of insight, not to mention that it absolves you of responsibility for your relationship difficulties. So you will continue paying him for his services. The fact is, however, you might have difficulty making commitments if your parents had not gone through a divorce and even if their marriage had been idyllic. If that was the case, however, the therapist would have simply "discovered" another connection, perhaps that you have difficulty making commitments because you don't think you can live up to your parents' example. My point is that these supposed cause-effect relationships are cut from whole cloth. They are untestable inventions, and arbitrary ones at that. Five therapists may well find five different "causes" for your problems, none of which can be verified.

Yes, one's childhood experiences have an influence on the adult the child becomes, but the influence is far from predictable. The child is *not* father to the man. Negative childhood experiences do not necessarily predestine adult problems any more than a wonderful childhood predicts a blissful adulthood. After all, a good number of people who grow up within adverse family circumstances manage, without the help of therapists, to make lemonade out of lemons. Likewise, a good number of people who grow up in highly advantageous family circumstances, raised by parents who would be considered exemplary by any reasonable standard, take a wrong turn somewhere and wind up trashing their lives. This wasn't their parents' doing; it was their own doing.

Ironically, Freud's most significant contribution to present-day parenting is guilt, infections of which tend to single out mothers. Because Freudian mythology has managed to stay alive despite a lack of proof, the all-too-typical modern mom believes that she is *cause* and her child's behavior is the *effect*. This belief has benefit only as long as one's child is behaving properly and doing well in school, but the downside of pride is a heavy load of guilt when behavior or grades suddenly go south.

Grandma Had It Right

Grandma knew that the most powerful shaping force in a person's life was the force of the person's own free will. She understood that the choices people, including children, made were *influenced* by early childhood experiences, socioeconomic factors, cultural expectations, peer pressure, and so on. But Grandma also understood that when all was said and done, people were fully responsible for the choices they made. Thus, when one of Grandma's kids did something wrong and tried to mount a defense, she turned her withering look on him and said, "There are no excuses—no ifs, ands, or buts." The Freudian point of view allows—even encourages—excuses, ifs, ands, and buts. Grandma would hear none of them. She held her children fully responsible for what they did, and she held them fully responsible from the time they were toddlers.

Grandma also knew that she could not be a good enough parent to guarantee that her children would never do anything despicable, disgusting, or depraved—that the power of their choosing was *more* powerful than the power of her parenting. She knew that to be the case because the Bible told her so.

Western civilization's first parenting story is contained in the third chapter of the book of Genesis. Its theme, in a nutshell: the only perfect parent there is or ever will be creates two children who disobey his first instruction. What, pray tell, did God do wrong that caused his first kids such pronounced *obedience issues?* Freud might have said Eve resented that Adam was created first, that he was obviously the favored child. Tempting Adam to eat of the fruit of the tree of knowledge was an expression of this resentment, a passive-aggressive means of lowering Adam's image in God's eyes. Grandma would have scoffed at this. She knew there was no psychology behind the Fall. It happened because human beings possess what animals do not: freedom of choice, including the freedom to choose wrongly. If a perfect God could not raise children who were perfectly obedient, what chance do you have?

The Adam and Eve Principle: *No matter how good a parent you are, your child is still capable on any given day of doing something despicable, disgusting, or depraved.*

It will be highly therapeutic if you read the previous sentence out loud, in the first person and present tense. (Out loud!) "No matter how good a parent I am, [insert your child's name] is still capable on any given day of doing something despicable, disgusting, or depraved."

Now, don't you feel a whole lot better?

That brings us to the first of humanist psychology's two contributions to Postmodern Psychological Parenting: the idea that children are fundamentally good; that in any given situation a child is inclined to do the right thing.

THE HUMANISTS BITE THE DUST, PART ONE

In the 1960s, new age gurus and mental health professionals developed various therapies and workshops that would supposedly help people get back in touch with their wonderfully innocent, playful, wise, and peace-loving inner children—the real, "natural" selves that had been forced into cowering exile by parents and teachers intent upon producing conformists who would willingly serve capitalist society (aka "the Machine"), which was thought to be the genesis of all evil. Unfortunately, the new age myth—*every child is an incarnate being of holy light, sent from heaven to grace us with his or her immaculate presence*—still thrives. Moreover, it has become the dominant cultural view.

It follows from this fairy tale that children do wrong things because their holy nature has been corrupted. And make no mistake, the mythmakers want you to believe that the number-one corrupting influence is bad parenting. So where parental guilt is concerned, if Freud doesn't get you, humanism will.

The Little Criminal

Grandma knew that every child came into the world bearing a nature that was already corrupt, depraved; that each and every child was a natural-born criminal; and that to steer the little criminal in a prosocial direction required a combination of powerful love and powerful discipline. She knew this because the Bible had told her so, and she had seen it with her own eyes.

The Bible is clear on the subject: Human nature is fundamentally sinful. Psalm 51:5 says we are sinful "at birth," from the get-go. Proverbs 22:15 tells us that "folly is bound up in the heart of a child." The Hebrew word that is here translated "folly" is used in other contexts to mean moral depravity. This means that in any given situation, a child is inclined to do the wrong thing, the self-serving thing, to consider his own interests before anyone else's.

The real, honest-to-badness human being—a raging sociopath (although often charming, like many sociopaths)—emerges from behind the deceptive mask of infancy sometime during the second year of life. The story is universal, and it always features a child whose behavior suddenly begins to reflect the three beliefs that form the core of the criminal/sociopath mind-set:

1. What I want, I deserve to have (entitlement).

2. Because I am entitled to what I want, the ends justify the means (pragmatism).

3. The rules do not apply to me; therefore, no one has a right to deny me or stand in my way (narcissism).

The metamorphosis is usually sudden, startling. One unremarkable night, parents put to bed an eighteen-month-old, who has been to that point cuddly, affectionate, and easygoing. The next morning when they walk into his bedroom, they are met by the Spawn of Satan, who announces that their parenting honeymoon is over.

The demon-child demands his way and screams like one possessed when his parents don't dance to his tune, don't dance fast enough, or dance the wrong dance. He also expects them to read his most royal mind and goes ballistic if they are lax in this duty. If they try to comfort him during these frequent fits, he slaps, scratches, and bites them. He blatantly defies their instructions while looking at them as if to say, "I dare you to do something about it." He seems impervious to punishment, demands to be served like a potentate, and is displeased by his parents' most conscientious attempts to serve him properly.

"Where has our sweet boy gone?" they wail.

They do not realize that the sweet boy they lived with for eighteen months was not the *real* boy. The real boy, the real human being, woke up at eighteen months, stepped out from behind the beguiling mask of infancy, and asserted, "I am!"[2] He realized, in a burst of insight, that he is "me," and the discovery is intoxicating. This is the same self, the same human nature that first awakened and asserted itself in the Garden, and the result has always been the same: disorder in the house. This disorder is exacerbated by the fact that during infancy and early toddlerhood, the child is the center of attention of parents who are waiting on him hand and foot. Under the circumstances, he has every right to believe that his parents exist for the sole purpose of serving him, to do his bidding. After all, he does not know that they preceded him, that there was life before the great and powerful "me" came into existence. Jean Piaget, the foremost developmental psychologist of all time, said that during the first two years of life a child is *egocentric*—he believes that the world revolves around him. Sinfulness and egocentricity are a highly explosive combination, as parents of toddlers will attest.

THE SAME THING SAID THREE DIFFERENT WAYS

Man is the measure of all things.
                    —*PROTAGORAS, CIRCA 440 B.C.*

No higher answer exists. We must construct it ourselves.
—*BIOLOGIST AND AUTHOR STEPHEN JAY GOULD, LATE*
                    TWENTIETH CENTURY

You're not the boss of me!
                    —*THE TODDLER, SINCE THE BEGINNING*

Raging Against the (Parental) Machine

The toddler is a factory of antisocial behavior. One does not have to teach a toddler to hit, steal, lie, disobey, covet and destroy other people's property, or act selfishly. Such behavior comes naturally to a toddler. This is exactly where psychological explanations of human behavior break down, because psychology cannot explain such things as the following:

One day, the mother of a twenty-month-old child who has never witnessed an act of violence, even cartoon violence, denies him a cookie before supper. The child falls to the floor and begins having a high-self-esteem seizure. His screams can be translated thusly: *"How dare you deny me, lord of the universe, a cookie! Give me the cookie or suffer the full force of my wrath, wretched underling!"* Out of the goodness of her heart his mother picks him up with the intent of comforting him, and with perfect aim and perfect timing he slaps her across the face. Believe me, the slap is not an accident, no random thrash that just happened to connect with mom's cheek. As a camera would have proven, the expression on the child's face at the moment of impact was pure, 100 percent demonic.

What is the psychological explanation for this outburst of violence directed at the very person who has shown this child the most kindness, who has sacrificed her own needs in order to meet his? What unresolved issue is the child attempting to express (Freudianism/humanism)? Who has modeled such vicious behavior for him (behaviorism)? And keep in mind, please, that violence is the stock-in-trade of the toddler. He slaps his mother, pulls the hair of other children (and if the smile on his face is an indication, he enjoys hearing them cry), pushes his younger brother to the floor just to see him fall and hear him wail, and appears to derive great pleasure from trying to pry people's eyeballs out of their sockets. Freudians, humanists, and behaviorists are struck dumb by toddler behavior of this sort.

God in his infinite mercy and grace has distinguished us from animals in many ways, but one is most significant to our discussion: He has not allowed human offspring to grow to full size in one or two years. Imagine the consequence to a mother who denies her five-foot-ten-inch-tall, 165-pound two-year-old male child a cookie before dinner. Not a pretty picture. God is good.

Likewise, psychology cannot explain why, as soon as a child begins to master the power of language, he begins to lie. (Most interestingly, the first lie told by every child is the first lie recorded as having been told: *I am not responsible for what has happened here; I'm not even responsible for what I did.* First Adam said this, then Eve.)

Psychology has no means of explaining why a child whose parents have been as loving and caring as parents can be suddenly begins to refuse to obey even the most innocuous of their instructions and seems to take perverse delight in doing exactly the opposite of what they ask of him. Psychology cannot explain the arbitrarily rebellious behavior of the toddler because psychology refuses to accept that humans are by nature rebels without a cause. That is the biblical perspective, and since Freud, psychology has taken the greatest of pains to distance itself as much as possible from anything "religious." After all, Freud wrote that belief in God was a delusion and religion was the refuge of the neurotic. In a sense, psychology is postmodernity's toddler, determined to deny that there is a Truth, an Authority, greater than itself.

The single biggest challenge of parenthood is that of socializing the toddler. That sometimes Herculean task demands discipline that causes the child to (a) realize he will not be able to get away with criminal behavior, even as a "baby," and (b) submit to the civilizing force of his parents' loving yet awesome authority. (But make no mistake, whereas the toddler may submit, he never goes away, and every so often, even well into adulthood, he demands to be heard, to be the center of attention, to be catered to, to be obeyed. You've seen other adults' toddlers suddenly burst forth, and if you are reasonably self-aware, you can even identify regrettable occasions when you let your own toddler take over and begin terrorizing the world. The new age gurus and humanist psychologists were right about one thing: The inner child is very real; he lives within each of us. He's the toddler that needs to sit in permanent time-out, preferably facing the corner.)

Grandma, who understood that her toddler was a criminal-in-the-making, stepped up to the plate and cured his criminality to the best of her ability (and make no mistake about it, this cure, however effective, is never complete). But then Grandma believed Psalm 51:5 was the truth. Today's parents are not curing toddlerhood, but then today's parents read Psalm 51:5 and are loath to accept that the reference is to their children.

> *Surely I was sinful at birth, sinful from the time my mother conceived me.*
>
> —*PSALM 51:5*

Reaching the Unteachable

But the delusion does not end there. When I ask an audience, "Does one have to teach a toddler to hit, lie, or disobey?" the answer that comes back is always "No!" All right so far.

Then I ask, "Is it possible to *teach* a child to be nonviolent, to tell the truth, and to obey legitimate authority?"

"Yes!" the audience answers.

Wrong! In order to teach, one must have a willing student, one who realizes his deficiencies and readily pays attention to the teacher. The fundamentally sinful toddler does not qualify, not by a long shot. The truth is that before one can teach a child the whys and wherefores of right behavior, one must *force* wrong behavior to stop. One must *force* a child to stop hitting, *force* a child to stop lying, *force* a child to stop stealing and destroying, *force* a child to share.

This force requires two things: parents who communicate to the child that they *will not tolerate* hitting, lying, stealing, and destroying; and consequences that are potent enough to form permanent memories.

I am reminded of one of our grandchildren, whose parents told my wife, Willie, and me, when he was two, that he hit them when things didn't go his way.

"How are you dealing with this?" we asked, to which they replied that they were explaining to him that hitting was wrong and trying to help him develop better ways of expressing frustration. In other words, they were trying to *teach* a toddler to stop hitting, not realizing that *force* was the prerequisite.

Several weeks later, said grandchild was spending the weekend with us while his well-meaning parents were out of town. While trying to dress him, I somehow incurred his displeasure. He promptly hauled off, emitted a savage yell, and slapped me across the face. I immediately reached around him and slapped him, with intent to cause significant pain, on his bare bottom— once. I didn't do this out of anger or some retaliatory reflex. I did it because I knew, as his young parents did not, that he had to be *forced* to stop hitting. His big blue eyes got even bigger, he began to quake, his mouth opened wide, and he started howling and jumping up and down, holding his bottom. I picked him up, held him close, and told him I loved him but was not going to let him hit me or anyone else. When he calmed down, I put him on a chair, knelt in front of him, and *taught*.

"What did you do?"

"I hih-hih-hit you," he answered, his sobbing not quite fully over.

"What did I do?"

"You spanked me!" he answered, with a tone that bordered on defiance.

"Yes, I spanked you," I said, "and the next time you hit me, I'll spank you again. And if you hit Grandma, I'll spank you. If you hit anyone in my house, I'll spank you. Do you understand?"

"Ye-heh-hes."

Then we talked about what I had done that he didn't like. (I finally figured out that I was telling him to step into his underwear, whereas his parents still placed him on his back and put it on for him.) I told him what to say when he doesn't like something. I taught for about two minutes—the attention span of a just-turned-two-year-old—and then got back to the business of dressing him.

Three weeks later, the parents proudly reported that said grandchild had suddenly stopped hitting! A miracle!

Once again, all I did was (1) make it perfectly clear that I was not going to tolerate hitting, and (2) bring to bear a consequence potent enough to form a permanent memory. (By the way, the next time this grandchild saw me, he ran up to me and jumped into my outstretched arms. Authority, legitimately exercised, slowly liberates the human spirit, which is creative and loving, from the prison of human nature, which is anything but.)

The Awakening

Parents who do not understand that the real human being is not the manifestation of holiness and innocence are in for a rude awakening when the Little Criminal awakens from the slumber of infancy and begins demanding that they please and obey him. Their lack of preparation enables the child to knock them off balance, a position from which some parents never recover. For that reason, I advise parents of infants to prepare themselves for the Little Criminal's bursting upon the scene, and when he does, to make it clear to him from day one that they do *not* exist to please him, that they are *not* going to obey him, that, in fact, it's the other way around.

A few years ago, an obviously distressed mom called my office and persuaded Willie to set up a phone consultation. Her twenty-month-old had awakened screaming from his midday nap four days earlier and had not stopped since. She and her husband had tried everything to get him to stop, but nothing had worked. Even giving him new toys caused him to scream even louder. If anyone tried to hold him, he began thrashing around as if he was in pain. He had even caused himself to throw up several times.

On the third day, now desperate and worried sick, the parents had taken him to the pediatrician, who, unable to determine a cause for the child's persistent howling, had referred him to a pediatric neurologist. The neurologist was also stumped and had scheduled him for an MRI. When I returned the mother's call, I could hear the child screaming in the background. Both sets of grandparents, an aunt and an uncle, and several friends had gathered at the home to console the now-distraught parents.

"Do you have any ideas, anything that could possibly help us?" the mom asked. I could hear her anguish. At several points during the ensuing conversation, she broke down in tears.

I had a sense of what was going on. The real human being had awakened, and for whatever reason, nonstop screaming was the way he had decided to announce his arrival. I related to the mother what I thought. It was certainly not the explanation she expected, but it definitely fit the facts.

"What should we do?" she asked.

I told her to take him to a comfortable sofa and place him in the angle between the back and a seat cushion, facing out. Then she was to sit down and move back against him, applying just enough pressure to keep him there, pinned in place. He should be able to squirm, I said, but not escape. While he was so pinned, Mom was to talk softly to him, telling him that it was all right to scream, but as long as he screamed, she was going to keep him there. Then she was to say positive things like "life is good, we live in a nice house, we eat good food, we can pay all of our bills, and America is still the greatest country on the planet." She didn't know it, but the real purpose of having her say such things was to help *her* calm down.

"You may have to hold him there for a couple of hours," I warned.

She thought that was no big deal, given that she had survived his screams for three days already. I told her to let him up when he stopped, but to stand ready to pin him to the sofa the minute he started wailing again. She assured me she would follow my instructions and call me with a progress report the next day.

As promised, she called the next evening. I immediately knew from her calm, confident tone that all was well.

"It was amazing, John," she said. "He screamed for about an hour and stopped, so I let him up. He started up again about an hour later, but I immediately went back to the sofa with him and he stopped right away. He hasn't screamed in nearly twenty-four hours. He's been playing contentedly and happily. I have my little boy back again!"

Several days later, another good progress report, and that was that. The moral of the story: How do you prevent a little sociopath from becoming a big, full-blown sociopath? Sit on him.

Had this mother not been willing to accept that her child's sinful nature had awakened, she and her husband might have fallen for the currently popular notion that any persistent behavior pattern that deviates ever so slightly from the norm is a sign of either psychological or physiological problems. Both of these explanations—which are really two sides of the same post-modern coin—deny the sinfulness of human nature, deny that even a toddler exercises free will, and deny that a child is (and should therefore be held) fully responsible for his behavior. These parents might have wasted years, not to mention thousands and thousands of dollars, pursuing a chimera. They would have begun, when their child was not yet two, ceding authority in his life to medical and psychological professionals who would have had a field day with his "case."

Said professionals would have ordered one test after another and come up with one hypothesis after another, each requiring yet more tests. Meanwhile, the parents' sense of powerlessness would have grown and deepened. They would have suspended serious attempts to discipline until the professionals found the reason for their child's behavioral problems. The behavioral problems would have worsened, therefore, and the psychologists and medical doctors would have collaborated on the stock diagnoses—attention deficit hyperactivity disorder, oppositional defiant disorder, bipolar disorder of childhood.

At that point, the pharmaceutical industry would have gotten in on the act. One prescription after another would have been tried. Some would have worked longer than others, some not at all, and to some the child would have had negative reactions, all of this "proving" that the child's case was unique.

And down the slippery slope of never-ending "treatment" this family would have gone. This is speculation, of course, but this is also a description of a reality being experienced by millions of parents and children today, and largely because we have forgotten about sin. (More about that later.)

THE HUMANISTS BITE THE DUST, PART TWO

Humanistic psychology's second contribution to Postmodern Psychological Parenting is the idea that high self-esteem is desirable—essential, in fact, to personal happiness—and parents should do everything in their power to help their children acquire it.

In the late 1960s, psychological propagandists began portraying high self-esteem as the holy grail of right and proper parenting. Nearly fifty years later, the propaganda continues unabated. Raise a child properly, parents are told, and your child will acquire high self-esteem. Parent improperly, and your child will implode psychologically. He'll grow up thinking he's a worthless piece of protoplasmic junk.

Supposedly, any negative response to a child's behavior or task performance will lower this precious psychic commodity. Praise boosts self-esteem, while punishment depresses it. Success (e.g., high grades, receiving a sports trophy) causes self-esteem to go up, while failure and disappointment (e.g., low grades, not receiving at least a "certificate of participation") cause it to go down. High self-esteem was supposedly the natural condition of the child, before the imposition of parental authority smothered it. All of this hoo-hah held great appeal for a generation of parents who, like my wife and me, had been raised on regular doses of "Because I said so." And so off we baby boomers went, down the yellow brick road to the Land of Parenting Oz.

Before going any further, let's accurately define the term self-esteem. "Self" refers to one's person. To "esteem" means to admire, worship, venerate, revere, and adore. To have high self-esteem, therefore, means to admire one's own person—to think highly of one's self.

Grandma didn't believe people should think highly of themselves. In fact, she did not have a lot of regard for people who did. She thought, and rightly so, that high self-regard was a problem, not a solution to a problem. Grandma valued humility and modesty and did her best to pass those virtues along to her children. "Don't brag," she told her children, and, "It's not polite to attract a lot of attention to yourself." When one of her children "forgot himself" and began getting carried away on the intoxicating breezes of high self-esteem, she sternly told him that he was acting too big for his britches and that he'd better get himself back down to his normal pants size, and quick. (Being on one's "high horse" meant the same thing.) In

Grandma's view, what we today call high self-esteem was something to be frowned upon, discouraged.

That's a biblical point of view. Scripture does not validate high self-esteem. In the Old Testament, every single person with high self-esteem takes a huge fall, self-destructs, or is the eventual recipient of God's wrath. In the New Testament, Jesus spoke on the subject of self-esteem—numerous times, in fact.

- "If anyone would come after me, he must deny himself and take up his cross and follow me" (Matthew 16:24).

- "The last will be first, and the first will be last" (Matthew 20:16).

- "For everyone who exalts himself will be humbled, and he who humbles himself will be exalted" (Luke 14:11). (It is significant to note that here Jesus was quoting almost word-for-word from Isaiah 2:12.)

During the Sermon on the Mount, in the Beatitudes (Matthew 5:3–12), Jesus blessed the "poor in spirit," "the meek," and "those who mourn." There is simply no way to square Jesus's teachings with the notion that high self-esteem is a good and wonderful thing that parents should pursue on behalf of their children.

Sometimes, a person will point out to me that Jesus also said to "love your neighbor as yourself" (Matthew 22:39). That's right, but it is a mistake to think Jesus was advocating self-love. That would make no sense in the light of his other comments (above) on the subject. If the statement is turned into a question—"Do you love your neighbor as much as you love yourself?"—the honest person would be forced to answer in the negative. In other words, Jesus was challenging us to accept that self-love is the stumbling block to sufficient love of one's fellow man. Rather than endorsing self-love, Jesus was saying that in order to love our neighbors as much as we should, we need to love ourselves less . . . much less. This is the same sort of challenge he issued when he said that a man who has even looked with lust upon another woman is as guilty of adultery as someone who has actually broken his marriage vows and had sex with a woman other than his wife. Let's face it: Jesus was inclined toward tall orders.

Violent Pride

For many years, I have contended that good social science research always confirms both Scripture and common sense, and indeed, such is the case here.

Social scientist Roy Baumeister has spent more than a decade studying people who possess high self-esteem. His results would come as no surprise to Grandma. Baumeister has discovered, for example, that people with high self-esteem tend to have low self-control, especially when they aren't getting their way. They don't handle defeat or disappointment very well. Why? Because people with high self-esteem think they are entitled to always be the winner, Numero Uno.

Furthermore, they tend to lash out, verbally and often physically, at the people they blame for their defeats and disappointments. Baumeister finds that wife abusers have generally high self-esteem, as do child abusers, people known for frequent episodes of road rage, and inner-city gang members.

Most stupefying, Baumeister discovered that hard-core criminals—people locked up in maximum-security prisons—score higher on self-esteem assessments than any other group. That should send chills up and down your spine.

> ## WRONG!
>
> *In one sense, high self-esteem is an insurance policy; it is our best guarantee that a child will make the most fruitful use of his capacities.*
> —*DOROTHY CORKILLE BRIGGS,*
> YOUR CHILD'S SELF-ESTEEM

When I share this with an audience, I often point out that Adolf Hitler had high self-esteem and, correspondingly, no regard for anyone else. So did (or does) Joseph Stalin, Osama Bin Laden, Saddam Hussein, Ted Bundy, and every other degenerate sociopath you can think of. Common sense says that the higher one's self-esteem, the lower will be one's regard for the rights of others, including, in extreme instances, their very right to life.

On the other side of the self-esteem spectrum are people such as Mahatma Gandhi and Mother Teresa—selfless individuals who think first and foremost about others. But there is no better example of selflessness than Jesus Christ, who had such love for us, so little regard for his own self-interest (actually, Jesus had no self-interest at all), that he willingly paid the price of our sins so that we might become citizens of heaven. Jesus

said in order to become his disciple, a person must first "deny himself." How much more explicit could he have been concerning the ultimate worthlessness of high self-esteem? After all, self-esteem and self-denial are polar opposites. To love God with all of one's heart and mind, one must put aside all forms of idolatry, including esteem of the self.

> *Then Jesus said to his disciples, "If anyone would come after me, he must deny himself and take up his cross and follow me."*
> —*MATTHEW 16:24*

Here is a summary, according to the best social science research, of the characteristics that typify people who possess an abundance of self-esteem:

- An overriding sense of entitlement ("What I want, I deserve to have")

- Low self-control, especially when frustrated

- Apt to explode toward others when they don't get their way

- A criminal/sociopath mind-set, distinguished by the belief that the ends justify the means

The reader should recognize those as characteristic of the toddler—the little criminal. Again, Grandma knew that high self-esteem was a problem, not a solution to a problem; that the problem first expressed itself in the behavior of a toddler; and that preventing a little sociopath from growing into a big one required a combination of powerful love and equally powerful discipline, which Grandma was not a bit reluctant to administer.

Self-Esteem Goes to School

The correspondence between high self-esteem and low self-control should resonate with any veteran elementary-school teacher. Over the past forty years, as promoting self-esteem has taken precedence over promoting academic excellence, the self-control of America's kids has taken a nosedive. Testament to this is the fact that whereas fifty years ago a single teacher had no problem controlling a first-grade class of forty or more children, today's first-grade teachers have their hands full with twenty-five, and today's teachers have aides! Yesterday's teachers dealt with the occasional behavior problem; today's teachers deal with an epidemic of kids with so-called "behavior disorders," all of which are variations on the theme of low self-control.

American education has led the way in the quest to find and fill the new Holy Grail. Despite a plethora of research showing that high self-esteem is undesirable, American education clings tenaciously to the myth that the higher a child's self-esteem, the better will be his school performance. That myth is belied by the steady drop in academic achievement levels over the past forty years. It is further smashed by research findings to the effect that individuals with high self-esteem perform consistently lower than predicted by their ability levels, not to mention lower than they *think* they're performing. That's because people with high self-esteem possess an entitlement mentality; they believe that *anything* they do is worthy of merit. As a consequence, they rarely do their best at anything.

Self-Esteem Goes to . . . Work?

This entitlement mentality is beginning to show itself in the workplace. A corporate manager recently told me, echoing many other managers and employers, "We're having lots of problems with this new generation of workers." A friend of mine recently told me that one of the prime reasons he is setting up a factory in Asia is that young people there possess what American young people are losing: a good work ethic.

"Why should I pay a twenty-five-year-old American kid ten dollars an hour for doing only what's required of him," my friend said, "when I can hire a twenty-five-year-old in India who believes in doing the very best job he is capable of doing and will work twice as hard for half the pay?"

(Please don't misunderstand me. I am not defending the practice of exporting jobs. I am pointing out the degree to which the quest for high self-esteem has damaged the national work ethic and threatens to tear down everything previous generations worked hard and sacrificed to build.)

> *Anyone who has dealt with college students in recent years knows that work is a declining value and practice in America.*
> —CLYDE WILSON, RETIRED PROFESSOR OF HISTORY, UNIVERSITY OF SOUTH CAROLINA[3]

Whenever I give a talk on the problems associated with high self-esteem, I'll see a good number of puzzled looks sprinkled throughout the audience. After all, over the past forty years the supposed virtue of high self-esteem has become taken for granted. So, when I say that high self-esteem is not a virtue, that it is a dangerous social commodity, parents often react with confusion sometimes bordering on distress, as if what I'm promoting will impair their children's ability to succeed in life. These imagined impairments take three predictable forms: that lacking self-esteem, their children will (1) not have what it takes to become leaders, (2) possess no self-confidence, or (3) become depressed. In fact, these imagined impairments are exactly that: imagined.

Good Followers

Concerning leadership, I point out to parents that they do not simply want their children to become leaders—they want their children to become *ethical* leaders. After all, some of the most effective leaders in history have been degenerate sociopaths—Hitler, for example. Ethical leadership is exercised in the best interest of others, not in the best interest of the leader himself. The ethical leader is focused on helping the people he or she leads bring out the best in themselves. Ethical leaders do not have high self-esteem. They have high regard for others. Unethical leaders have high self-regard and low regard for others. In their view, other people exist to help them reach *their* goals; to be manipulated, at best, or eliminated, at worst.

Besides, why do nearly all parents want their kids to be leaders? What is so awful about being a good follower? Is good leadership better than good followership? If so, then why? Is it because good leaders make more money than good followers? Is it because they enjoy more social status? I suggest that what parents really want is for their children, as adults, to find ways of contributing to the common good to the best of their ability. If the best of their ability involves leadership, that's fine. But if the best of their ability is followership, well, that's fine, too. Given that, as the number of leadership positions is limited, most children will be followers, not leaders, perhaps parents would do best to help their children learn to be good followers. That learning begins in the home, by the way, with chores and obedience and good manners.

Nor is a high level of confidence in one's own ability necessarily a good thing. Researchers have found that people with high self-esteem regularly overestimate their abilities, to their ultimate detriment. Because they are so sure of their superiority, they are likely to approach tasks, especially challenging ones, without having invested adequate effort in practice and preparation. Therefore, they are likely to perform less well than people with lesser ability and lesser self-confidence who, realizing their shortcomings, do their homework. High self-confidence can also cause people to take foolish, if not downright life-threatening risks. In the final analysis, it's not the person with high self-confidence who is most likely to succeed in life; it's the person who possesses a realistic appraisal of his or her strengths and weaknesses.

Concerning depression, some research suggests that people with high self-esteem may be more likely to suffer depression than people who lack self-esteem. People with high self-esteem have little tolerance for disappointment, frustration, failure, and criticism. These everyday facts of life often send "high self-esteemers" into tailspins, invoking the "flight or fight" (depression or aggression) principle. (Whether the response to circumstances that threaten the self-evaluation of a person with high self-esteem is depression or aggression seems to be a matter of personal history, situational variables, and personality.) It's as if people with high self-esteem epitomize the axiom "the higher they fly, the farther they fall." The opposite of high self-esteem, then, is not depression. The opposite of high self-esteem is humility—characteristic of both good leaders and good followers.

Wrong Again!

High self-esteem is . . . the essential core, the basic foundation, of positive mental health.
—*THOMAS GORDON, PH.D.,* TEACHING CHILDREN
SELF-DISCIPLINE AT HOME AND AT SCHOOL

THE BEHAVIORISTS BITE THE DUST

It is no coincidence that people who embrace a mechanistic view of the universe—people who believe, on faith, that the universe came into being accidentally and that evolution explains the unique appearance of life on Earth—also embrace a mechanistic view of human behavior.

In the 1960s, as the psychological parenting revolution was gearing up, the behavioral theories of psychologist Burrhus Frederic (B. F.) Skinner burst out of academia and into popular culture. Skinner believed that the same simple principles that govern the behavior of rats, dogs, and other animal species also govern the behavior of human beings. That is, behavior that is rewarded strengthens, and behavior that is not rewarded or punished weakens and eventually "extinguishes." Smitten with the idea that the behavior of a child could be altered as easily as a rat's, psychologists began proclaiming that it was just a matter of time before parents skilled in the use of behavior modification would be raising a new generation of blissfully well-behaved, high-achieving mod-children. Some forty years later, parents are experiencing more problems in the discipline of children than Grandma even thought possible.

Inconsequential Consequences

What went wrong? Quite simply, human beings are not animals. As recorded in the book of Genesis, we are God's special creation, created for relationship with him. It is ludicrous to think that a mechanistic approach to the manipulation of behavior will work equally well on animals and humans. The idea presumes that animals and humans are different only in that *homo sapiens,* quite by accident, came out ahead in the evolutionary slog.

Unlike animals, human beings possess free will: We are capable of resisting the power of consequences. Rats and other animals are not capable of such resistance; they bend involuntarily to the power of any consequence. Unlike animals, humans are rebellious by nature, something animals are not. Humans are the only species that regularly engages in acts of self-destruction. A human being will sabotage his own best interests to prove that the rules don't apply to him, that he is impervious to any and all attempts to make him change his ways. Thus the ubiquity of the parental complaint, "My child keeps right on doing what he wants no matter what I do to him." Dog trainers do not make this complaint; nor do rat trainers. In my graduate school course in experimental psychology, twenty-four students were given twenty-four rats and told to teach them to run mazes. All twenty-four students employed the same behavior modification techniques, and all twenty-four rats learned to run their mazes equally well. If twenty-four sets of parents, guided by twenty-four behavioral psychologists, use the same set of behavior modification techniques on twenty-four misbehaving children, eight of the children will get better, eight will get worse, and eight will stay about the same. (I didn't make that up, by the way. These numbers reflect the research findings concerning the results of psychological therapy.)

Consider: A rat comes to a choice-point in a maze, where it can go either right or left. If it goes to the right it will be rewarded with a morsel of cheese, but a left turn will result in a slight electric shock. Said dumb beast will venture to the left only two or three times before it will never, ever go left again. But given a choice between "going to the right" and being rewarded or "going to the left" and being punished, a human may well go to the left over and over and over again just to prove that no one has authority over him, rules do not apply to him, and he is immune to discipline. As the toddler so eloquently puts it, "You're not the boss of me!" Or as the teen puts it, "I don't care what you do to me!"

A man spends ten years in jail for robbing a convenience store at gunpoint. He is released, and four months later he is back in jail for robbing a convenience store at gunpoint. This is not because "the system failed him" or some such blather, but because he is a toddler at heart. He's no different from the toddler who keeps right on pulling the dog's ears even though his mother pops his behind and puts him in his crib for ten minutes following every single pull. Does he like being spanked and confined to his crib? No, not any more than the criminal likes being in jail. But in both cases the narcissistic need to prove that the rules don't apply, that the only authority in the child's/criminal's life is the child/criminal, cancels the effect of the punishment.

Unrewarding Rewards

It turns out that when it comes to humans, reward is no more reliable than punishment. Rewards sometimes have a paradoxical effect on human behavior. Take, for example, a five-year-old who seems to enjoy tripping his younger brother. After determining that punishment doesn't work, his parents decide to reward him if he doesn't trip his brother for one hour. An hour goes by with no tripping, and the parents give the child some candy along with lots of praise and then are dismayed to discover that the tripping actually increases! It's as if the child figures out that the way to get his parents to offer him candy is to trip his younger brother. Kids are a lot smarter than rats, after all. Researchers have also found that praising and rewarding children for a job well done—say, coloring—may cause certain children to stop performing altogether!

With a dog, correct consequences will result in correct behavior, but all bets are off with a human being. If a dog does the wrong thing, and its trainer does the right thing, the dog will stop doing the wrong thing. But if a child does the wrong thing, and his parents do the right thing, the child may keep right on doing the wrong thing. A dog does not possess free will; a child does. This means that a child will change his behavior only if he *chooses* to do so. A persuasive enough consequence may promote the right choice, but because the child is a human, not an animal, there are no guarantees. Correct consequences change the behavior of a dog. Correct *choices* change the behavior of a human being.

Behavior modification seems to work often enough on children (that is, children choose to cooperate with it just often enough) to make parents and teachers believe that if they just tweak it properly or apply it more consistently, it will work all the time. But that simply isn't the case. To paraphrase Abraham Lincoln, you can fool some children with behavior modification some of the time, but behavior modification will not fool most children very much of the time at all. Behavior modification also seems to work fairly well with children who have serious developmental delays and in closed, institutional settings, such as residential treatment centers for incorrigible youths. But in the field, in real life, it only "works" as often as children *choose* to comply with it.

Unfortunately, most of today's parents have bought into the myth of behavior modification. Over the past forty years or so, behavior modification has become the reigning disciplinary paradigm. When parents use the term "discipline," they usually mean some means of manipulating reward and punishment. The belief that what works with rats and dogs also works with human beings is why the discipline of children has become overwhelmingly frustrating and stressful.

Once upon a time not so long ago, parents understood that for the most part, the discipline of a child was accomplished by simply meaning what one said and saying exactly what one meant. If, for example, a parent told a child he could not have a candy bar, then it was necessary that the parent stick to her guns and demonstrate to the child that no amount of persuasion or distress would obtain the candy bar. Furthermore, most folks understood, and intuitively so, that discipline was fundamentally a matter of leadership, not punishment-ship or consequence-ship. As we will soon see, it still is! There is, after all, nothing new under the sun.

The Postmodern, Psychological Point of View	Grandma's Point of View
Freudian: Early childhood experiences shape behavior and personality.	Biblical: The child's behavior is influenced, but not *determined* by outside influences; rather, the child *chooses* his path in life.
Humanistic: Children are fundamentally good.	Biblical: Children are fundamentally sinful.
Humanistic: High self-esteem is good and parents should help their children acquire it.	Biblical: Modesty and humility in all things is desirable; furthermore, those with high self-esteem "will be humbled."
Behavioral: Behavior modification works on human beings as well as it works with rats and dogs.	Biblical: Humans are not animals. Possessing free will, humans can successfully resist the manipulations of behavior modification.

UTOPIA BITES THE DUST

Enough time has passed to determine whether this grand social experiment is working or not. Is it? One single fact answers the question: Since 1965, when Postmodern Psychological Parenting began gaining a toehold in our culture, every single indicator of positive well-being in America's children has been in a state of precipitous decline. Today's children are nowhere near as happy as kids were just two generations ago.

"Oh, come on, John," a psychologist once retorted, "there is no happiness measure. You're just making that up!"

No, I'm not. And yes, as I pointed out to him, there is a happiness measure: the per-capita rate of child and teen depression, which has increased at least fivefold since 1965. In just one fifteen-year period, from 1980 to 1995, the suicide rate for boys ages ten to fourteen almost doubled![4] If that's not unhappiness, I don't know what is.

I grew up in the 1950s. Ironically, my peers and I were expected to shoulder more responsibilities than are kids today, and our parents and teachers expected a lot more of us than is the case today, yet we were much happier than are today's kids. The high school I attended in suburban Chicago was huge: some four thousand students in 1965. In four years, in a mega–high school, I knew of no one who committed suicide. No one took razor blades and carved satanic symbols or weird messages on their arms or engaged in any other form of nihilistic self-abuse. There was, of course, the occasional kid who wasn't the happiest of campers, but no one was so incapacitated by unhappiness that he or she had to drop out of school or enter residential treatment (it was called by less politically correct terms back then). Don't get me wrong. I'm sure there were kids with problems. They were few and far between, however. In today's typical high school, by contrast, many of the girls are taking antidepressants, a good number of kids are into self-mutilation, lots have regular appointments with therapists, thousands of dollars are being spent annually on suicide prevention, and the dropout rate is climbing, even among the middle and upper-middle classes.

It is not arguable: America's kids were a whole lot happier before parents began listening to psychologists (and remember, I am one!) and other mental health professionals. Am I saying that my profession is the problem? Yes, I most certainly am. Mental health professionals were the prime architects of Postmodern Psychological Parenting; therefore, they are primarily responsible for the damage it has caused.

It is not arguable: Today's parents are having more problems with their children than their parents and grandparents thought possible, experiencing more stress than did all of their ancestors combined, and yet they have more professional advice at their disposal than ever before. That's not irony; it's cause and effect. The advice is the problem.

Grandma's advice wasn't perfect. Grandma was human, and nothing humans do or dispense is perfect. But Grandma's advice worked. It worked for the child, the marriage, the family, the school, the community, and the culture. It worked then, and as attested to by a growing number of parents who have unplugged from PPP and plugged themselves back into Grandma's wisdom, it still works.

Postmodern Psychological Parenting is a house built on sand. It's been crumbling from the day its front door was first opened to the public. We abandoned the house built on rock some forty years ago. The good news is it's still standing, and it's as livable as ever. Grandma still lives there, in fact. Stay with me if you'd like a tour.

Questions for Group Discussion or Personal Reflection

1. Identify three aspects of your child's performance or behavior, whether positive (good grades) or negative (disruptive behavior), about which you have tended to feel either prideful or guilty. Consider the possibility that your child would be doing the same things if he'd been raised by someone else. How would your parenting behavior be different if that was in fact the case?

2. Have you tended, at times, to make excuses for your child's misbehavior? If so, give an example. How would your parenting behavior differ if you did not allow "ifs, ands, or buts"?

3. Are you willing to accept that your child's free will is more powerful than your parenting? Give three examples of behavior on the part of one of your children that bears no relationship to how you have raised him, where you have obviously done your best and yet your child continues to do his "worst."

4. Were you knocked off balance when your child's real nature first emerged? Are you still off balance when it comes to discipline? If yes, in what ways? How does it change your parenting perspective and attitude to accept that your child's nature inclines him to do the wrong thing in any given situation?

5. Consider: What was the point of Jesus's redemptive sacrifice on the cross if all antisocial behavior is the result of either unresolved psychological issues or physiological "imbalances" and the like?

6. Identify several high-self-esteem behaviors that your child exhibits on a frequent basis. Examples are tantrums, interrupting conversations, being loud and disruptive, pouting, and refusing to obey. Have you tended to make excuses for some or all of these behaviors (e.g., "he's just four years old," "he'll outgrow it") and failed to adequately discipline your child?

7. Identify several of your child's misbehaviors that have seemed impervious to discipline—nothing you've tried has worked. How do you imagine your parents or grandparents would have dealt with these same problems? Would they have used behavior modification? Would they have had the same degree of frustration?

8. Rank order, in terms of influence, the following factors that are involved in the behavior of a child: parenting, peers, temperament, miscellaneous events and circumstances in the child's life, free will, God's will. Discuss with the group and see if consensus can be reached.

CHAPTER THREE

The Serpent's Currency

Oh, I believe in yesterday.
—PAUL MCCARTNEY, 1965

Although they claimed to be wise, they became
fools. . . . They exchanged the truth of God for a lie and
worshiped and served created things rather than the
Creator.
—ROMANS 1:22, 25

One of Grandma's favorite parenting aphorisms was "good citizenship begins at home," which simply means that at all times, and in all things, parents should "aim" their child rearing at the goal of producing a good citizen, a person of value to the culture. In this regard, Grandma understood that she was raising an adult, not a child. This is also the meaning of Proverbs 22:6: "Train a child in the way he should go, and when he is old he will not turn from it."

GRANDMA'S THREE RS

In Grandma's day, home and family were a character-education classroom in which parents were teachers and children, students. Within this classroom, parents developed and delivered a curriculum designed to teach children a set of values essential to good citizenship. The core of this curriculum was composed of the following "Three Rs":

- *Respect* for the fundamental dignity of every human being, which children develop by first learning respect for people in positions of legitimate authority, beginning with their parents.

- *Responsibility* in two equally important senses of the term: first, accountability for one's own actions; second, a willingness to carry out tasks assigned by authority figures (as well as those that are simply due the family/community by virtue of one's membership within it).

- *Resourcefulness*—a hang in there, tough it out, try-and-try-again attitude brought to the challenges of life.

From this threefold core emanates all of the more specific attributes of good character. Honesty, for example, derives from personal responsibility and respect for others. Charity comes about when people recognize their responsibilities to the larger community, and especially to those less fortunate. Charity acknowledges the dignity of every human being, regardless of his or her station or circumstances. And so on. Frugality, compassion, industry, self-restraint—they all have their genesis in the three Rs.

A cord of three strands is not quickly broken.
—ECCLESIASTES 4:12

"Grandma's Home School Character Curriculum" was a powerful and uplifting experience, for sure. She endowed her children with *respect* for others by teaching them good manners, and from an early age. She taught *task responsibility* by involving them in household responsibilities. She insisted that her children accept accountability, or *social responsibility,* for their behavior. Finally, by expecting them to solve their own problems, entertain themselves, do their own homework, and even devise their own playthings, Grandma all but ensured that her children would develop a *resourceful* attitude toward life's challenges. In this last regard, it is important to note that Grandma believed she should do *as little as possible* for her children, thus helping her children learn to stand on their own two feet.

Grandma's practical, commonsensical, down-to-earth, biblical approach fell by the wayside as Postmodern Psychological Parenting captured America's attention. Because of the emphasis on providing children with success experiences, training in good manners was slowly but surely replaced by training in skills, and chores were replaced with after-school activities. The new psychological paradigm also enticed parents into thinking that the parent who does the most for his or her child is the very best parent of them all. As for accountability, Grandma expected her children to fight their own battles, lie in the beds they made, and stew in their own juices. All too often, today's parents are found fighting their children's battles, lying in beds their children have made, and stewing in their children's juices.

Grandma was determined that her children would learn good manners, which are demonstrations of respect for others. A child who practices his manners is slowly engraving respect for others on his or her heart. Grandma understood that respect for *others,* not high *self-*esteem, defines the emotionally healthy, prosocial individual. She also knew that in the course of treating others with respect, a person slowly develops a sense of personal dignity, or self-respect—the sense that he or she is making a positive contribution.

RESPECT YOURSELF

Don't be fooled! Self-respect and self-esteem are not, as many seem to think, synonymous. They are actually polar opposites. Self-respect develops as one treats others with respect and dignity, no matter their station. As respect is given away, self-respect grows within. This creates a constant "feedback loop"—as one treats others with respect, self-respect develops, thus enhancing one's respectful treatment of others, and so on. In the vernacular, "What goes around, comes around."

On the other hand, a child develops self-esteem not by giving, but by getting. Self-esteem develops courtesy of people who do things for the child, create success experiences for him (even false success experiences), and praise him, as well as courtesy of things he does for himself. As self-esteem grows, respect for others diminishes. Self-respect is synonymous with a generous heart, while the heart of a person with high self-esteem is subjugated to selfishness.

People with high respect for others (and therefore, high self-respect) are fulfilled no matter their status, salary, or state of material wealth. High self-esteem, on the other hand, creates the illusion of self-fulfillment. It creates a craving for attention, recognition, status, dominance, and things, no amount of which is ever enough.

> *A proud man is seldom a grateful man, for he never thinks he gets as much as he deserves.*
> —*HENRY WARD BEECHER (1813–87),*
> *AMERICAN CLERGYMAN AND SOCIAL REFORMER*

A person with self-respect focuses primarily on his or her obligations to *others*. For a person with high self-esteem, it's all about what other people can and should be doing for *him*. A person with high self-respect does the best job he can because his sense of personal dignity will allow no less, and by doing a good job, he contributes to the well-being of others. A person with high self-esteem only does a good job if he thinks it will advance his first cause—himself. High self-esteem is a form, therefore, of idolatry—where the self becomes one's personal god. The word "esteem" is, after all, synonymous with "worship."

Self-respect exists independent of status. It is the knowledge that you are making a positive contribution, and not just from nine in the morning until five in the afternoon, five days a week. It is the knowledge that you are making a positive difference in this world every time you stop to let another driver in front of you, open a door for someone, give your seat to an elderly person—every time, in other words, that you treat someone else with dignity and courtesy. Self-respect is not about how much money you make, the size of your house, how much your cars cost, or how physically attractive you are (by secular standards); it's about the real, authentic *you*. It's about character, and a person's character shines through not in his possessions or his status, but in his or her manners, his treatment of others, even others he doesn't know and may never see again.

When all is said and done, *the fundamental difference between self-respect and self-esteem is the difference between wanting to do for others (looking for opportunities to be of service), and wanting/expecting others to do for you (wanting to be served).* As I said earlier, these two attributes are polar opposites; they define people who are fundamentally different and therefore different in every way. Quite obviously, self-esteem is not the biblical ideal.

MANNERS TAKE A BACK SEAT TO SKILLS

As did most children of my generation, I went to first grade not knowing my ABCs, but I knew my manners. Before I was six, my mother (a single parent for most of the first seven years of my life) had taught me to address adults as "sir" or "ma'am," to say "please" and "thank you," and to open doors for women and the elderly. Mom trained me to be attuned to the presence and needs of others.

Today's parents would *say* they are trying to teach their children good manners, but their efforts are obviously sporadic at best. Fundamental things seem to escape their attention.

For example, eight months a year, I spend a good amount of time on the road, traveling from one speaking engagement to another. I've lost count of the number of times I have ridden an elevator down to a hotel's first floor and been unable to exit effortlessly because as soon as the door has begun to open, children have started piling in, blocking my exit. Often the kids in question are teenagers, and in many cases their parents have been standing right behind them but have said nothing. Sometimes, the parents have entered right behind the children! And there I am, trapped, trying to be heard as I ask, "May I please be allowed to get off?" On more than one occasion, I've simply resigned myself to my peripatetic fate and taken another elevator ride.

It doesn't take a lot of time or effort to train children to proper elevator etiquette. All one has to do is say, "When the door opens, we stand aside while people exit, and we don't get on until everyone who's getting off has done so." My mother trained me to do that before I was five years old, before I went to school. When I ask someone my age when he or she learned to stand aside as people exited an elevator, the usual answer is, "I can't remember. I've just always done it." That means the learning took place early, as it did in my case.

Today's kids barge into conversations as thoughtlessly as they barge into elevators. It's somewhat understandable, given that many of today's parents seem to think that it's okay for a child to interrupt as long as he blurts out "excuse me!" beforehand. I met a fellow from South Africa a few years back who remarked on how often American children interrupt. He told me that in his country, children are trained from an early age to stand a respectful distance from adults who are talking to one another until there is a pause in the conversation. Is the child allowed to jump into the pause? Absolutely not! At the pause, an adult will turn to the child and ask, "Can I help you?" At that point, the child is allowed to speak. This fellow told me that children are trained to do this as early as three. How civilized! Instruction of that sort produces children who think of others first, themselves second. A child who is not trained in such fundamental courtesies is being allowed to think primarily of himself. He's being allowed to wallow in high self-esteem. Today's parents have been seduced[1] into thinking that's a good thing. I hope I've convinced you by now that it's anything but. It's a bad thing, a very bad thing.

Trophy Children

Yesterday's parents taught manners; today's parents tend to be focused instead on helping their children acquire skills, especially academic and athletic. This shift has occurred because skills are associated with high self-esteem; manners are not. I sense that many parents are trying to create what I call "trophy children"—children who, for example, know their ABCs at three and can correctly identify all fifty state capitals by the time they are four. So, instead of using the preschool years to build the foundations of good character, many of today's parents use the preschool years to try to jump-start their children's academic success. That works . . . sort of.

Compared to the fifty kids in my first-grade class, today's kids enter first grade with far better skills, but far less respect for adults. Interestingly enough, however, when parent education and income levels are held constant, kids in the 1950s performed at much higher levels in every subject area and at every grade than do today's kids. That's because children who respect adults pay attention to and obey adults, and children who pay attention to and obey their teachers will do their best in school.

The National Education Association and other public education propaganda groups have succeeded in convincing the public that smaller classrooms result in better learning. Hogwash! Since the 1950s, two first-grade statistics have declined: the teacher/pupil ratio and the average reading level attained by the end of the school year (those two declines are true at every grade level). In other words, and contrary to the myth, smaller classrooms have nothing to do with better learning. Everything else being equal, a good student is first and foremost one who pays attention in class. Children who come to school having learned to pay attention to adults (and especially female adults) will do far better than children who come to school not having learned to pay attention to adults. Smaller classrooms are not going to solve the attention deficits that so many children are bringing with them to school these days.

Teachers know the score. To make the point about manners,

respect, and good behavior, I will sometimes ask all of the teachers in an audience to stand. Then I'll say, "If you would rather teach a class of twenty-five kids whose IQs are 150 and above, but who are lacking in good manners, than twenty-five kids whose IQs are average but who are well-mannered and therefore well-behaved, please remain standing." Every teacher sits down. That says it all, doesn't it?

CHORES TAKE A BACK SEAT TO AFTER-SCHOOL ACTIVITIES

When I ask parents to identify the family activity that takes up most of their time, many name going to their children's after-school sports practices and events. I'm sorry, but watching a child play a sport and cheering from the sidelines does not constitute a family *activity*. A picnic is a family activity, as is a nature hike, spending the afternoon in a museum, or going to Niagara Falls or Dizzy World; cheering from the sidelines as one's child plays a sport does not qualify.

A family is also engaged in a truly *family* activity when everyone pitches in to clean the house, weed planting areas, or plant a garden that teaches good stewardship and helps put food on the table. Sadly, few of today's families can be found doing those types of things on any sort of regular basis, if at all. What with all the after-school activities the kids are involved in, not to mention homework, there's just no time. I contend, therefore, that many children are growing up without an adequate sense of what "family" really and truly means. They know what the word "team" means, but they do not know that one's family is the greatest team one can ever be a member of.

A child learns how to be a family-team player by having a meaningful role, consisting of meaningful responsibilities, within his family. That role and those responsibilities should be defined before a child is four years old and expand as the child grows. In the course of performing chores, a child contributes to his family. He develops not only a sense of personal value but also a sense of his family's value to him. His bond to his family grows ever stronger as does his bond to the values the family holds dear.

Home Work

Unfortunately, most of today's kids are making no meaningful contribution to their families. Occupying a bedroom, watching television, playing video games, and consuming family resources are not acts of contribution, and that, unfortunately, is the full extent of many a child's "role" in his or her family. Another way of describing this nouveau state of affairs is to say that in today's all-too-typical family, the only persons who are acting as if they have obligations are the parents.

The problem with this one-sided state of affairs is that consumption without contribution inevitably engenders a feeling of entitlement, the feeling that "I deserve." Under the circumstances, individualism (high self-esteem) and materialism begin to rule, hobbling the development of more functional prosocial values as well as a truly valid sense of self-worth, based on a knowledge of God's love.

The child so hobbled ends up feeling okay when he is getting what he wants and not okay when he is not getting what he wants. Ironically, the ubiquitous effort to make children happy is putting them at risk for becoming perpetual malcontents. It has no doubt played a significant role in the steady rise in the rate of child and teen depression since the 1960s when "you can go outside after you've finished your chores" began its slide into obscurity, to be replaced by "hurry up, we've got to get you to football practice on time." Until a child is emancipated, his consumption within his family is always going to outweigh his contribution to his family. But parents can and should make the effort to strike the greatest degree of parity between them, to ensure that the child does not grow up believing that it's possible to get something for nothing.

In the 1950s and before, nearly every child in America was trained to the obligations and responsibilities of family citizenship with a curriculum of household chores. Boys and girls began performing these chores as early as age three. Before I was four years old, for example, my mother taught me to wash floors. That I wasn't able to do as good a job as she would have done was beside the point. Although she expected me to do my best, Mom understood that the quality of my floor-washing was secondary to the fact that I was giving back to our little family— I was making a contribution. In the process, I was absorbing the good citizenship ethic, expressed as follows by President John F. Kennedy in his 1961 inaugural address: "Ask not what your country can do for you; ask what you can do for your country." Likewise, being a good citizen of one's family means asking *not* what your family can or should do for you, but what you can and should be doing for your family.

By the time I was five, Mom had taught me to wash my own clothes in her washing "machine"—a galvanized tub with hand rollers bolted to it. By the time I was ten, my job every spring was to wash the interior walls of our house and re-oil the exterior cedar trim. By age thirteen, I'd learned how to paint a house, replace broken window panes, care for a lawn, wash and iron my own clothes, prepare a garden for planting, and cook a full meal. My experience was by no means unique. It was, in fact, the norm for kids in my generation, many of whom grew up on farms and performed more service to their families than a city boy like me could even imagine.

Today's parents say things like "I *try* to get my children to do chores." That means the children do chores sporadically, only when leaned on by Mom or Dad, which means Mom and Dad have failed to make the doing of chores a priority. Something else I hear: "I'd like my kids to do more chores, but there's hardly any time what with after-school activities and homework." But that begs the question: Why do so many parents think after-school activities are more important than doing chores? I suggest that when all has been said about "learning how to be a team player" and "developing good social skills," the *real* reasons that chores have been replaced with extracurricular activities are (1) chores are not associated with success and self-esteem, and (2) everyone else is doing after-school activities.

In that second regard, a significant number of parents have told me they're concerned their kids won't develop good social skills if they aren't involved in after-school activities. I think that's baseless.

First, truly good social skills are founded on respect for others, and I can't say it loudly or often enough: Respect for others is taught through manners, not how to kick a soccer ball.

Second, kids in my generation who grew up on farms and didn't have much contact with kids outside their families except in church developed good social skills. I can attest to that because I went to college with lots of young people who'd grown up on farms. To be honest, many of these kids had better social skills than kids who'd been raised in crowded suburban neighborhoods. (In the final analysis, a person with high respect for others is going to have much, much better social skills than a person with high self-esteem.)

Third, to any parents who really wants to help their child improve his or her social skills, I say, "Then turn off the television, get rid of the video games, and remove the personal computer from your child's bedroom!" Nothing dampens a child's social skills more than solitary, mind-numbing electronics. I'm in danger, at this point, of beginning to rant one of my favorite rants, so let's go back to the subject at hand. (For anyone interested in my tirade on the effect electronic media are having on today's kids, see chapter 6 of *The NEW Six-Point Plan for Raising Happy, Healthy Children* [Andrews McMeel, 2006].)

Take This Job

A growing sense of entitlement among young people is undermining the American work ethic. That's attested to by managers who tell me that many young adults coming into the workplace have the attitude that the employer-employee relationship is pretty much a one-way street, that it's the employer's responsibility to do things for them—to pay them a hefty salary, to provide a laundry list of benefits, to let them have time off whenever they want it, and so on. Many a young employee seems to think his or her responsibility ends with coming to work (but not necessarily on time) and doing just enough to get by.

A friend of mine, a manager with Bank of America, tells the following story: An employee in his division was entering incorrect figures into the database. When my friend pointed this out, the young man—a college graduate—shot back that his job description didn't say he was supposed to enter *correct* data. He maintained that it was someone else's responsibility to check his work and make whatever corrections were necessary. When my friend tried to explain that that wasn't how it worked, the young man stormed off in a huff and complained to another supervisor.

I'll bet that young man grew up in a home where next to nothing was required of him. Like most young people of his generation, he probably played on lots of after-school teams, but he never learned the right stuff of being a family-team player.

That story may represent the tip of the iceberg, but stories of that general sort are by no means exceptional. Over the past five years, a good number of sole proprietors have told me they do not hire people below the age of forty. One such employer recently told me he was no longer hiring people below the age of fifty, and his minimum age requirement was increasing by a year every year. Amazingly enough, he was only thirty-eight!

"Too many people younger than me have little if any respect for authority," he told me. "People older than me, however, seem to have respect for authority even when the authority—in this case, me—is younger than they are."

These stories attest to parents who are making more effort to promote high self-esteem than good citizenship. The effort has obviously succeeded. After all, it takes an abundance of self-esteem for a person in his early twenties to tell a forty-something supervisor that he's right, the supervisor's wrong, and if the supervisor doesn't like it, too bad.

ACCOUNTABILITY FALLS TO "INVOLVEMENT"

Before the psychological parenting revolution of the late 1960s, parents expected their children to accept full responsibility for their mistakes and misdeeds. Expressed in the vernacular of the day, parents expected children to fight their own battles, lie in the beds they made, paddle their own canoes, and stew in their own juices. This translated thus:

- **Fighting your own battles:** A child who came home complaining about a teacher was told by her parents that if she knew what was good for her, she would stop acting in ways that incurred the teacher's displeasure and do everything possible to get the teacher to "like" her. Her parents further promised her that if she failed at that assignment, and the lack of success was reflected on her report card, she would not like the consequences.

- **Lying in the beds you make:** The parents of a child, a generally good student, who failed to study for an important test and was subsequently barred by the school from participating in a day-long field trip, refused to go to the school and take up his defense. They let him "take his licks."

- **Paddling your own canoe:** The father of a teenager refused to help him design and construct a competitive science project on electromagnetic energy, telling his son that as much as he wanted him to do well, he would have to do well on his own. The father, a physicist, pointed out that by giving help, he would be giving his son an unfair advantage, which he could not ethically do.

- **Stewing in your own juices:** A ten-year-old let another child ride his new bicycle for a day. The child parked the bike in a public place, and the bike was stolen. The ten-year-old child's parents not only refused to say anything to the other parents, they also refused to buy him a new bicycle, telling him he must earn the money himself.

Those were not fictional tales. They came from people my age and older. In every case, the adult in question said that the experience, however painful at the time, was one of the most character-building episodes of his or her life. Notice that in each case, the parents in question do *not* get involved with their child's conflicts, responsibilities, and problems. They expect the child to stand on his or her own two feet.

Overinvolved and Overstressed

Postmodern Psychological Parenting seduced parents into a high-involvement style of parenting. Today's parents believe that the more involved they are in their children's lives, the better parents they are. All too many of today's parents, confronted with the same issues described above, would be likely to

- **Fight the child's battles:** A child comes home complaining that her teacher doesn't like her. The parents go to the school and confront the teacher, accusing her of causing their child to have a "negative educational experience." Any attempt on the teacher's part to defend herself is ignored, even rebuffed. Any attempt on the teacher's part to explain that the child is a behavior problem in class is denied.

- **Lie in the child's bed:** A child fails to study for an important test, knowing that a passing grade is necessary to participate in an upcoming day-long field trip. The child fails to make a passing grade. The parents go to the school and complain to the principal that excluding their child isn't "fair," and that his self-esteem is going to suffer if he isn't allowed to go on the field trip. They even imply that if the principal holds his ground, they may hire an attorney.

- **Paddle the child's canoe:** A teenager who wants to win an award at an upcoming science fair asks his father, a physicist, for help. The father ends up designing and building the science project while the teen sits and watches. It never occurs to the father that he's giving his child an unfair advantage. In his mind, his involvement is testament to his desire to be the best father he's capable of being.

- **Stew in the child's juices:** A ten-year-old lets another child ride his new bicycle for a day. The other child parks the bike in a public place, and the bike is stolen. The parents call the other child's parents and demand that they pay for the bicycle. When the other child's parents offer only to split the cost, the ten-year-old child's parents get angry, hang up, and promptly go out and buy him an even better bicycle.

How is it that today's parents, raising two kids, feel more stress than did parents of fifty years ago who were raising five kids? How is it that the latter felt hardly any stress at all? A large part of the answer is that the more parents feel they have to get *involved* in their child's lives, the more stress they're going to experience. It's just that simple.

Hovering Parents

In the 1980s, in my newspaper column, I began using the term "helicopter parents" for parents who hovered over their children, micromanaging every conceivable detail of their lives. These parents help their children with their homework, manage their social lives, arrange their recreation, and generally go to bat for their kids whenever their kids encounter any sort of problem. It appears that once a helicopter, always a helicopter. In November 2006, the Associated Press released the following blurb:

> **Helicopter Parents Hit the Job Market:** College admissions counselors and student life staff have begun developing policies for working with "helicopter parents"—those over involved parents who hover all around the lives of their young adults, scheduling their classes, settling roommate disputes, etc. Employers now say those same "helicopters" are showing up at job fairs and even at interviews with their kids. In the most extreme cases recruiters say parents will come to job fairs even without their kids, talking to potential employers and even calling after an interview to find out why their son or daughter did not get a particular job. Parents say they worry about the motivation and capabilities of their children and are therefore trying to help them land those first jobs.[2]

No one in my generation had parents who were "helicopters" of that sort. At least I've never run into anyone my age who describes parents that even come close to that description. Having "overprotective" parents back then meant they checked to make sure you'd done your homework (but did not check your homework) or wouldn't allow you to ride your bike more than a mile from your house. That's small potatoes compared to accompanying an adult child to his first job interview.

The difference is that the traditional paradigm encouraged minimal involvement. Thinking back, I realize that my job as a child was to *keep* my parents from getting involved in my life. I did that by "takin' care of business." If I behaved myself in school, did the work I'd been assigned, and did my best, my parents *didn't* get involved in my school life. If I behaved myself in the community, did what other adults told me to do, and treated adults with respect, my parents *didn't* get involved in my life outside the house. And what a wonderful thing that was, for them and me both! As long as I did what I was supposed to do, I enjoyed a tremendous amount of freedom. And the more freedom I enjoyed, the more freedom my parents enjoyed. The low-involvement paradigm benefited both parents and child in that way.

The new, high-involvement paradigm means that children are rarely free of their parents, and parents are rarely free of what they think their obligations are to their children. Within this setup, children become dependent upon their parents' involvement, and parents begin to measure their success as parents by their children's accomplishments. Today's generally high level of parent involvement in homework is a prime example. The more involved parents become in a child's homework:

1. The more they take the child's grades personally, as a measure of the success of their involvement.

2. The more convinced the child becomes that he can't succeed in school without their help, and the more dependent he becomes on their involvement.

3. The more involved the parents become and the more dependent the child becomes, and the more helpless he acts, the more convinced the parents become that their involvement is necessary to their child's "success."

And around and around it goes. This describes many of today's parents. Furthermore, it describes codependency. Codependent relationships are addictive. They're like quicksand: They suck people in, and people get stuck in them. The above AP story is testament to the fact that parent-child codependency is rapidly becoming the norm in America. This is bad. It's bad for children, but it doesn't stop there. It's bad for parents, and it's bad for their marriages; it's bad for schools, communities, and culture. Parent-child codependency bodes very, very ill for the future of America.

More than anything, America needs another parenting revolution. Actually, America needs a retro-revolution in parenting—a revolution that restores things to the way they once were, not so long ago. The longer we allow the new psychological paradigm to fester, the more problems it's going to create for all concerned, and the more difficult it's going to be to bring about that revolution.

Are you willing and ready to become a revolutionary?

Questions for Group Discussion or Personal Reflection

1. On a scale of one to ten, rate each of your children with regard to the following three attributes: respect for authority, willingness to accept responsibility, and resourcefulness. What could you do to increase those ratings? How might your parents have rated you when you were your child's age? List five essential differences between their parenting style and yours.

2. Have you spent as much time and effort teaching good manners as you have making sure your children's skills are up to par? What fundamental manners do your children lack? What has gotten in the way of your children's manners education?

3. Is each of your children a good citizen of your family? For each child age three and older, make a list of household chores he or she is capable, with some training, of doing reasonably well. Put a check mark beside those chores the child is actually doing. If all of the chores are not checked, what has gotten in the way of your children's good citizenship education?

4. How much time would be freed for truly family activities—nature hikes, visits to museums, picnics, family board games, and so on—if your children were not participating in *any* after-school activities? What, if anything, prevents you from cutting the time your children spend in after-school activities by,

say, half, and using that time to strengthen your family?

5. Identify several recent occasions on which you lay in a bed one of your children made, fought one of your children's battles, paddled a child's canoe, or stewed in a child's juices. Imagine what would have happened if you had not done those things. What would your child have learned if you had not solved the problem for him or her? Would the ultimate benefits have outweighed the pain?

6. Who is more susceptible to peer pressure—you or your child?

CHAPTER FOUR

The Tower of Parent-Babble

That is why it was called Babel—because there the
LORD confused the language of the whole world.
—GENESIS 11:9

On May 8, 2007, Amazon.com listed 49,314 book titles under "parenting." Mind you, that's the number of parenting books that were *in print* on that date. It does not include the thousands of parenting books published in and since the 1960s that are no longer in print. If these 49,314 books were stacked one atop another, and we postulate an average per-book thickness of one inch, the resulting stack of books would be 4,109 feet high! That is more than twice the height of the Sears Tower in Chicago, which is the tallest building in America at 1,450 feet. That is twice the height of the Freedom Tower at the World Trade Center, currently under construction but projected at 1,776 feet, including its spire. This imagined stack of books, which I call "The Tower of Parent-Babble," began growing in the 1960s, and American parents have been held in its sway ever since.

If the number of parenting books isn't daunting enough, consider the range of topics. In the child-care section of a typical megabookstore one finds books on how to raise every conceivable "type" of child: adopted, difficult, bipolar, anxious, oldest, middle, youngest, only, shy, gifted (usually sold out), ADD, ODD, OCD, and on and on and on it goes. Mental health professionals, with their penchant for making children and child rearing seem as complicated as complicated can possibly be, have created the impression that in order to raise a child properly, one must first know what "kind" of child one has. If a parent cannot figure that out on his or her own, a mental health professional will be glad to help.

JUDGING THE BOOK BY THE COVER

Grandma knew that each child was unique to some degree, but she also knew that the "sameness" shared by all children far outweighed their differences. Every child ever born, save one, has brought the same nature into the world, and that nature, and that nature *alone,* defines how children should be reared (save children with serious physical or mental disabilities, which do not include such things as ADD and learning disabilities).

The cacophony emanating from the Tower of Parent-Babble has convinced today's parents that "individual differences" define parenting; that each category of child requires its own highly unique, customized approach. This has caused the parents of, say, adopted children to believe not only that they must master "adopted parenting," but also that no one but other parents of adopted children can understand their children's needs and what those needs demand.

The trend toward stressing individual differences is further testified to by the multitude of parent support groups that have sprung up all across the landscape, each a place where parents of a certain type of child can bond for comfort, encouragement, and mutual assistance.

Scripture is relevant to every place and every time. When our early ancestors, who all spoke the same tongue, began building the Tower of Babel, the Lord punished them for their presumptuousness by confusing their language so that they could no longer understand and communicate effectively with one another.

> Now the whole world had one language and a common speech. As men moved eastward, they found a plain in Shinar and settled there. . . . Then they said, "Come, let us build ourselves a city, with a tower that reaches to the heavens, so that we may make a name for ourselves and not be scattered over the face of the whole earth." But the Lord came down to see the city and the tower that the men were building. The LORD said, "If as one people speaking the same language they have begun to do this, then nothing they plan to do will be impossible for them. Come, let us go down and confuse their language so they will not understand each other." . . . That is why it was called Babel—because there the LORD confused the language of the whole world. From there the LORD scattered them over the face of the whole earth. (Genesis 11:1–2, 4–7, 9)

Likewise, there was a time in America, and not so long ago at that, when everyone "spoke" the same child-rearing "language." Mothers and fathers, grandparents, teachers, neighbors, and shopkeepers were of one point of view when it came to children. Everyone was on the same page. This cultural consensus was slowly shattered as the Tower of Parent-Babble rose higher and higher into the sky, eventually blocking out the light and truth of the scriptural point of view. Where there had been one standard by which children were raised, there were now dozens of standards, each a variation on the theme of individual differences. Today's kids are rarely seen as simply children; rather, they are regarded through the filters of their supposed unique needs. Symptomatic of this is the way people use new child-rearing terminologies. For example, it is typical for the parent of a child who has been diagnosed with attention deficit disorder to say "My child *is* ADD," as if that one trait defines the entire child. He's no longer a child; he's a diagnosis. We do not say about someone who has been diagnosed with cancer that "he *is* cancer," yet certainly cancer is more significant to how a person should be treated than the fact that he or she has a shorter-than-average attention span.

Confusion Reigns

Today it is rare to find even a mother and a father who are on the same page where their children are concerned, much less parents and teachers or parents and grandparents or parents and neighbors.

In today's family, parents are likely to fight more about raising children than any other single issue. Fifty years ago, if a teacher called a parent to report the misbehavior of a child, the parent thanked the teacher for the report and punished the child. Today, a teacher makes such a call with great trepidation, for today's parent is likely to come to the child's defense and even blame the teacher for the problem. The adult unanimity that once prevailed concerning children has been shattered, and if there is one word that describes parenting in today's America, that word—right out of Genesis 11—is *confused.* Ironically, the more confused today's parents become, the more they turn to the Tower of Parent-Babble for answers, not realizing that it is the very source of their confusion. And the more confused they become.

Where there is confusion, there is also anxiety and stress, and indeed, today's parents are confused, anxious, and stressed about nearly *everything.* They are confused, anxious, and stressed over how and when to toilet train, how to deal with tantrums, how and when and even where to put their kids to bed, how and when and for what to discipline, what and where and when to feed their children, how much to expect of their children, how to talk to their children, how and when to say no, what to buy their children, what not to buy their children, what to let their children watch on television, whether to let their teenagers have their own passwords to the Internet, what to do when their teens are found to have been drinking or using drugs—as I said, *everything.*

Grandma was not and would not have been confused, anxious, or stressed about any of this—she would not have had any problems at all dealing with those issues. She took her child-rearing counsel from the Bible and her elders (who had taken their child-rearing counsel from the same sources); therefore, Grandma knew where she was "going" with each of her children, and she knew how to best get there. The Bible, God's Word, is not confusing.

People confuse themselves, mostly because they turn away from God and begin believing that man has all the answers—that "man is the measure of all things."[1] Today's parents, because they worship at the man-made Tower of Parent-Babble, because they have turned away—often unwittingly—from God's very succinct and uncomplicated instructions concerning child rearing, are not clear on their objectives. It is equally true to say that the objectives themselves are not clear; they are fuzzy. As a consequence, all too many of today's parents really do not know where they are headed with their children—they're making it up as they fumble along.

WHAT? OR WHY?

Because the Bible told her so, Grandma was primarily concerned with her children's *behavior.* In her view, the behavior of a child was an expression of his or her character. Misbehavior was an indication that the child's character education was incomplete or worse, lacking.

Even a child is known by his actions; by whether his conduct is pure and right.
—PROVERBS 20:11

Because conduct is verifiable, and because adults in Grandma's day were on the same page, authority figures trusted and supported one another where children were concerned. So, when a teacher or neighbor called a parent to report a child's misconduct, the parent assumed the report was valid and punished the child at home. In many cases, the child was not even allowed to tell his or her "side of the story" (likely to be a clever misrepresentation). A responsible adult had made a report about the child's behavior, and that was that.

That consensus began to unravel as the psychological view of the child replaced the biblical view. As its main theme, the psychological view proposed that a child's *feelings* were the standard by which adult behavior should be guided. Effectively, if a child doesn't like something, adults shouldn't do it, and vice versa. In *Parent Effectiveness Training*, psychologist Thomas Gordon, PPP's primary architect, wrote that parents should not set limits because, "Children hate to be denied, restricted, or prohibited."[2] Elsewhere in the same tome he says, "Treating kids much as we treat friends or a spouse . . . feels so good to children because they like so much to feel trusted and to be treated as an equal."[3] This sort of child-centered, touchy-feely claptrap would be laughable had it not been taken so seriously by so many.

Postmodern Psychological Parenting postulated that when a child misbehaves, the feelings that supposedly lie behind and drive the behavior are more significant than was the behavior itself. One of the mantras my graduate school professors drummed into me was that misbehavior on the part of a child was nothing more than a sign of underlying emotional distress, an indication that the child was struggling with an "issue" or "conflict" that was preventing him from behaving properly. (Note that this presumes that the child does not possess free will; he is a leaf being blown through life by psychological winds over which he has no control.) Punishing the misbehavior, therefore, might cause the child, out of fear, to suppress the misbehavior, but would cause the *real* problem to fester inside the child's psyche. In the long run, the child's problems would become even worse. Here's an example:

A five-year-old who is being physically hurtful to his two-year-old brother is really trying to tell his parents that he is angry at them for having another child before his own security needs had been fully met. He does not actually want to hurt his brother, but he lacks the language skills with which to tell his parents what is truly bothering him. Furthermore, he fears that if he expresses his anger directly at his parents they will reject him, so he expresses it by tripping, hitting, pinching, and taking things away from his sibling. If his parents punish him for this, the cruel behavior might stop, but his insecurity and therefore his anger at them will only become that much more pronounced. In fact, if the parents suppress the cruel behavior, which serves as a vent for his rage at his parents, the pressure of the psychological problem will just build up inside him and might eventually express itself in even worse ways—setting fires, perhaps.

That is the sort of pseudointellectual nonsense I learned to spout in graduate school. Note that in the above example, the so-called *real* problem is, in fact, entirely theoretical. Theories about behavior are not real. They are speculations, and while such speculations may be intellectually impressive, there is no way to verify whether they are correct. Behavior is real. Behavior can be objectively verified. Concerning the above example, the following are *real* statements:

- A five-year-old male child is terrorizing his two-year-old brother.

- He is acting toward his younger brother in deliberately hurtful ways.

- He knows he is causing his brother pain.

- The two-year-old cannot defend himself against his older brother's assaults.

Those statements are verifiable. People can agree on them. Agreement is far less likely when theoretical psychological motives are extrapolated from behavior and become the issue. Two psychologists may not even agree on them. One psychologist might say the five-year-old is acting out his anger at his parents. Another might say the five-year-old isn't really angry; he's just suffering from childhood bipolar disorder and therefore only *acting* as if he's angry when the real problem is a biochemical imbalance. A third psychologist might say that the older sibling doesn't know he's causing his brother pain; he's really trying to show him affection, but he's become anxious because of what he interprets as his parents' disapproval, and his attempts are therefore clumsy. (This is why, when parents who've seen a psychologist ask me if they should get a second opinion, I usually reply, "Get at least ten, and don't believe any of them.")

Psycho-Think

Unfortunately, all too many of today's parents are doing what I learned to do in graduate school. They engage in what I call "psychological thinking" concerning their children's misbehavior. Instead of viewing a given misbehavior as simply an error that needs to be corrected through the application of proper discipline, today's parents *interpret* it. "What does it *mean*?" they ask, and go on to ascribe some psychological significance to it. The misbehavior is thus transformed from a concrete event to an abstraction that embodies some supposed symbolic significance. It becomes shrouded in mystery.

The tendency toward psychological thinking on the part of today's parents was brought to mind by a mother who asked to speak with me just before a talk I was to give somewhere in America. With great concern, she told me she thought her seven-year-old son was depressed. She wanted to know if I could refer her to a professional. I asked how she had come to the conclusion her son was depressed. She told me he was "constantly negative about everything." When she fixed his breakfast, for example, he would sullenly grumble that her cooking stank. I asked for another illustration.

"Oh, well," she replied, "he complains about everything—the restaurants we choose, the clothes we buy him, the neighborhood we live in, his teachers, everything. He's never happy or satisfied."

I told her that she wasn't describing depression but rather rude, self-centered behavior—weeds that needed to be yanked unceremoniously from her son's behavioral garden and replaced with a patiently done planting of good manners and respect for others. I didn't think he needed a therapist; rather, he needed some good old-fashioned discipline. I went on to give her some suggestions for the ruthless "weeding" I hope ensued.

Before this mom can weed her child's garden, however, she is going to have to weed her thought processes where his misbehavior is concerned. As it is, she looks at him through psychological filters that only obscure the reality of what he is doing. Ultimately, she is confused, anxious, and guilt-ridden (she fears she may be a contributor to, if not the cause of, his supposed depression). She is, furthermore, unable to act because she worries that anything she does might lower His Regal Rudeness's self-esteem.

After giving a talk in Duluth, Minnesota, I was asked by a mother if I could help her understand why her eight-year-old son was hitting her on a fairly regular basis.

I asked, "What is there to understand?" to which she replied, "Well, I mean, I need to understand why he's so angry at me, right?"

Wrong. She needed to *act*, not understand. The only thing this mother needed to understand was that by trying to understand the psychology behind her son's hitting, she was transferring responsibility from her son to herself.

"An eight-year-old boy is hitting his mother" says that the boy is acting outrageously and needs to be disciplined. "An eight-year-old boy is hitting his mother because he is angry at her" says that the *mother* needs to be disciplined. She is doing something she shouldn't be doing, something that is making her son angry. The psychological explanation also justifies the boy's assaults on his mother. He is hitting her because he doesn't know how else to tell her that he is angry. Suddenly, the son who is hitting is the victim and the mother who is being hit is at fault. That's crazy!

Unfortunately, that is the very sort of craziness that accompanies psychological thinking. Every single time—not some of the time, but every single time—parents assign some theoretical psychological cause to a child's misbehavior, several consequences become inevitable:

1. *The child is no longer responsible for what he is doing.* A parent, both parents, or some other agency—teacher, peer group, or some circumstance in the child's life (the parents' divorce, the death of a favorite grandparent) is responsible. More often than not, the responsible party is the parent—in the parent's own mind, at least. More often than not, the child's mother ends up feeling most, if not solely, responsible, as in guilty.[4]

2. *The child is transformed from someone who is misbehaving into a victim of circumstances that are beyond his or her control.* Instead of discipline, he warrants compassion.

3. *The child's behavior is justified by the circumstances in question.* Suddenly, he is innocent of wrongdoing. He doesn't really *mean* to do what he is doing. His behavior is being driven by psychological forces that are beyond his ability to comprehend or cope with.

4. *The parents' ability to discipline is paralyzed.* How can a parent punish a child for doing what he can't help doing?

5. *Because they cannot bring themselves to punish the child, the parents become unwitting accomplices in and enablers of the child's antisocial behavior,* so the child's behavior becomes progressively worse over time. All too often, this culminates in an appointment with a mental health professional, a diagnosis, drugs, and long-term (read *expensive*) therapy.

As I said, this is crazy, nuts, flaky. It's nonsense. Ironically, this crazy, nutty, flaky nonsense has come about because psychology has held sway in American child rearing since the late 1960s. Even more ironic is the fact that precisely because they have been successful at causing American parents to think in crazy, nutty, flaky, nonsensical ways about their children's misbehavior, mental health professionals tend to make a lot of money.

DROWNING IN THE RIVERS OF BABBLE-ON

The disunity and confusion brought about by the Tower of Parent-Babble infected the very heart of the family, having to do with a fundamental difference between women and men: Women are creatures of great emotional depth and sensitivity, while men are most definitely not. There are, of course, exceptions to this general rule, but it is a general rule nonetheless. Because Postmodern Psychological Parenting stressed the importance of understanding and adjusting one's parenting behavior to children's feelings, the new parenting books resonated with women, while men found them difficult to relate to. Women read the new books and shouted "Yes!" while men read them (if they were forced to do so by their wives) and wondered "Huh?"

Men could not understand why, for example, they weren't supposed to just lay down the law with their kids; why instead they were to explain, reason, and compromise. Men wondered why they weren't supposed to simply punish their children when they misbehaved. After all, their fathers had punished them, and they were better off as a result. It did not escape their wives' notice that men had a difficult time getting on board the new PPP bandwagon, so for the first time in any culture at any time, women became wary of their husbands' participation in child rearing. This wariness was exacerbated by neofeminist propaganda to the effect that men were natural aggressors—that they maintained dominance by physically intimidating and abusing women and children.

Micromanaging Moms

Mothers began to feel that the weight of the entire parenting project was on their shoulders. They began to believe that whether their children turned out well was completely up to *them*—that a positive parenting outcome was a matter of *their* efforts, *their* energy, *their* dedication, *their* devotion. There was, furthermore, a new aspect to the job: to wit, doing everything possible to ensure that their children's feelings were not disturbed, and when they were, to do everything possible to set things right again.

As the weight of this responsibility settled on the shoulders of America's moms, they began to obsess about the details of child rearing, and the more they obsessed about detail, the more responsibility they felt, and the more responsible they felt, the more they obsessed about detail, and so on. Obsessing goes hand in hand with worry and guilt and so it became. For the first time in history, women began to feel that the terrain of child rearing was filled with psychological landmines that one untoward move on their part could set off, causing potentially irreparable damage.

Obsessive, worrisome moms began micromanaging their children, doing what micromanagers, wherever they are found, do: hovering over and racing around, checking on this and checking on that, fixing this and fixing that, making sure of this and making sure of that, helping with this and helping with that, arranging this and arranging that. Moms also began looking over the shoulder of anyone and everyone who had anything to do with their children, including their husbands, making sure these people were doing the "right" things.

Mind you, in the pre-1960s traditional family the mother was the "front-line parent," but those mothers did not feel that child rearing was their exclusive domain or responsibility. Rather, it was a responsibility shared by their husbands. As such, it was usual for mothers to consult their husbands when it came to most child-rearing decisions.

By contrast, today's moms rarely consult their husbands concerning such decisions. They simply make them and inform their husbands later, maybe. In many of today's families, in fact, the unspoken understanding is that Dad has little if any decision-making authority when it comes to the kids.

Mom can make decisions without consulting Dad, but Dad does not have permission to make decisions without consulting Mom—in which case, the decisions are ultimately Mom's. In fifty years, "Father Knows Best" has become "Dad Knows Next to Nothing."

The Incredible Shrinking Father

The typical modern father is on the periphery of child rearing. He has little if any decision-making power and even less disciplinary authority. As his wife orbits around the child or children, busily attending to ever-smaller bits of minutiae, the father stands outside the periphery of her orbit, awaiting instruction. He is, in effect, his wife's "parenting aide," whose function is akin to that of a teacher's aide in a classroom. The teacher's aide doesn't really know the curriculum, and neither does Dad, and Dad, like the teacher's aide, is there to simply assist the "real" parent and fill in for her when she needs a break. Even then, however, he can't be trusted to know what to do. He must be given a list of instructions.

Today's mother, when asked how many children she has, will often include her husband in the count. This is supposed to be funny, but it isn't. It is a sad comment on the fact that the role of father has diminished considerably over the past fifty years. In today's family, Dad takes instruction from Mom, as if he's one of the kids, and likewise, he requires supervision.

Ironically, many fathers are now cooperating in their own shrinking. One sign of this is the fact that many of today's dads come home from work with the intention of playing with their kids. When I ask a father why he does this, the typical reply is,

"I haven't seen my kids all day." That's true, but so what? This same man has not seen his wife all day either, yet he feels it's more important that he play with his kids than that he spend time in relationship with his wife. This strongly suggests that the all-too-common American dad has entered into a peer-to-peer relationship with his kids. Indeed, the new ideal in American fathering is to be best buddy to one's child. Unfortunately, that may be the only role a dad can play with his children without running the risk of censure.

David Blankenhorn, the author of *Fatherless America,* says that American fathers are slowly but surely becoming "feminized"—that instead of modeling traditional masculine virtues, they are acting more and more like second mothers to their children. Where the American father was once a disciplinary powerhouse, he is now a disciplinary milquetoast; like his wife, he's more concerned with his children's feelings than he is with their behavior. Ten years ago, most fathers expressed dismay at the touchy-feely manner in which their wives were approaching disciplinary issues. Today, both husband and wife are likely to be disciplining with kid gloves, doing two things that Grandma most definitely did not do:

1. **Trying to talk children into behaving properly.** I call this "yada-yada discipline"—generally fruitless conversation about misbehavior aimed at helping the child in question understand why he should not have done what he did and come up with better ways of behaving next time. The child's role during these therapeutic talks is to act as if he's taking it all in and to nod when the parent asks, "Do you understand?"

2. **Trying to discipline without hurting feelings.** When Grandma disciplined, she was *trying* to hurt her child's feelings; she was *trying* to make her child feel guilty. Grandma understood that unless emotional pain was associated with misbehavior, misbehavior would continue unchecked. But then, in Grandma's day, misbehavior was not a psychological phenomenon. It was sin, and one could not afford to fool around where sin was concerned.

Ten years ago, moms were often found running disciplinary interference between their husbands and their children—fearful that if they let their husbands discipline, psychological horror would result. Ironically, I am now encountering more and more women who actually complain that their husbands are the pushovers when it comes to discipline. I suspect this is the case because an increasing number of dads have entered into buddy-buddy relationships with their children and are concerned, consequently, with what their children think of them. Today's dads are giving up the good fight, or so it would seem. In any case, the disciplinary unity of husband and wife—once taken for granted—has been replaced by disunity and a confusion of roles.

And the Tower of Parent-Babble keeps babbling on.

Questions for Group Discussion or Personal Reflection

1. Do you tend to see your children through the filters of "individual differences" and respond to them primarily on that basis? How would your parenting change if instead of emphasizing your children's individuality, you viewed each of them as embodying the same sin-oriented, rebellious, self-centered nature that every child, from the beginning, has brought into the world? (Keep in mind that this nature is expressed differently by each child [*personality*], but it is nonetheless the same nature.)

2. When a teacher, neighbor, or friend informs you of misbehavior on the part of one of your children, do you tend to accept the report or do you tend to become defensive? If the latter, in what ways does your "parenting point of view" cause you to identify with and take personally what your kids do and do not do? What can you do to diminish that sense of identification?

3. Give an example of when you have engaged in psychological thinking concerning misbehavior on the part of one of your children. How did that thought process affect your ability to discipline? Did you make excuses for the child? Did you blame someone else, in whole or in part, for what your child did? What would you have done if you lived, say, one hundred years ago, before parents began to ascribe

psychological causes to misbehavior? Would you have disciplined more effectively?

4. Are you and your spouse on the same page when it comes to the children? Are your expectations the same? Are your messages to your children the same, and especially messages sent concerning misbehavior? If not, consider that one of you has adopted a "psychological perspective" on the children and the other has not; that one of you is more concerned with their feelings than their behavior. How would it affect the children if neither of you embraced the psychological perspective, if both of you focused exclusively on how the children *behaved*? Would that benefit them or harm them in some way?

5. Have you entered into what amounts to friendship with your child? Are you concerned with maintaining your child's approval? If so, how does that affect your ability to correct misbehavior? Were your parents your friends? If not, were you always confident that they loved you? What social forces have pushed you toward being a friend-parent?

PART TWO

Recovery

The infection of Postmodern Psychological Parenting is not so far gone as to be incurable. The bad news is that America will not be able to recover from its debilitating effects overnight. The good news is that parents can begin ridding themselves of the infection any time they choose. The disease is systemic, but recovery will be made one parent at a time. This section and the one following, on discipline, contain the prescription.

CHAPTER FIVE

Parenting as One Flesh

For this reason a man will leave his father
and mother and be united to his wife,
and they will become one flesh.

—GENESIS 2:24

Genesis 2:24 is the record of the moment when God, after he created man and woman, established marriage as the foundation of the family, the child-rearing unit. It is the first family principle. Before a married couple begins having children, for them to be one flesh means they should be devoted and faithful to each other. That means in the sexual sense, of course, but it also means that no other relationship or enterprise of any sort should come before their relationship with each other.

After they begin having children, for them to be one flesh means—listen up!—*no other relationship or enterprise of any sort should come before their relationship with each other*. In other words, being one flesh with children means the same thing as it does without children. The relationships a husband and wife have with their children should not, must not, come before their relationship with each other, and the enterprise of being parents (parenting) should not, must not, come before the enterprise of being married. Husband/wife must trump father/mother.

With that in mind, and after having read Genesis 2:24 out loud, I will ask parents in a seminar audience to answer the following question: "Of the time you spent in your family during the past week, what percentage was spent in the role of father or mother versus the percentage you spent in the role of husband or wife?"

The typical distribution is 90 percent parent versus 10 percent spouse, which is the empirical definition of a child-centered family. If in fact the first figure is above 50 percent, the family is child centered. The right answer to the seminar question above is no less than 60 percent wife/husband, and no more than 40 percent mother/father, and that's acceptable only during a child's infancy, when parenting demands are unusually high. Ideally, the relative percentages should be 75 percent spouse, 25 percent parent. A 90/10 skew in the other direction means that the typical American marriage is in danger of getting lost (if it isn't already) in the frenetic and rather constant child-rearing tango. That's simply not the way God planned it.

To repeat what I said in Chapter 1, *if you depart from God's plan in any area of your life, you will experience more (and more serious) problems than you would have encountered otherwise.* In this case, we're talking about the single most important of God's instructions to married couples! The nearly universal violation of this one instruction is sufficient to explain the profusion of child-rearing problems today's parents are experiencing. Keep in mind that many of the problems in question were relatively unheard of before the rise of Postmodern Psychological Parenting (e.g., tantrums and defiance beyond toddlerhood, children hitting their parents, blatant disrespect of adults, teen self-mutilation).

PARENTING FROM WITHIN THE MARRIAGE

One reason—perhaps the primary reason—the American family worked better in the 1950s and before (all of the available statistics bear this out) is that most married people with children, *even those who did not subscribe to the Bible,* were married first, parents second. The mother of fifty-plus years ago was a wife first, a mother second. Likewise, the father of fifty-plus years ago was a husband first, a father second. When the pre-1960s husband came home from work, he came home to be with his wife, who began preparing for his homecoming in the middle of the afternoon. She began cooking the evening meal, made sure the house was neat and tidy; she might have even bathed and changed from her housekeeping outfit into clothing that was more "wifely."[1] This ensured that when her husband came home from work, he was greeted not by his children's mother and not by the housekeeper, but by the woman he married.

After dinner, the children cleaned up the kitchen and dining area while Mom and Dad retired to the living room to talk or just relax together. The evening was not child centered, any more than was the family. The children understood that when their chores were done, they were to find things with which to occupy themselves, including their homework (in which their parents did not participate).

This arrangement and those understandings underscored the primacy of the marriage. The two adults in the household wore the hats of husband and wife far more than they wore the hats of mother and father, thus creating and maintaining a family that was marriage centered. Furthermore, the marriage operated the family. It was the family command post. Although the female adult was on the front lines of child rearing, the marriage raised the children. *That's* the way God planned it.

Wait Until Your Father Gets Home

For the marriage to raise the children means husband and wife are of one flesh, one mind where the children are concerned. They see their children through one set of eyes, adhere to one child-rearing plan (God's), aim at one set of goals, share one set of values, and act as one body when it comes to loving, teaching, and disciplining their children.

Parents whose child rearing fits this description can be said to be "parenting from within their marriage." The wife is a mother, yes, but she "mothers" from within her role as wife, with primary consideration of the unity she shares with her husband. When, for example, a child asks her permission to do something, and she isn't sure what her husband would say, her proper response is, "I'll talk about that with your dad when he gets home." If the child says the decision needs to be made right away, that when Dad gets home is too late, Mom's proper response is, "Then the answer is no." (If that sounds really odd, it's because you're under the age of fifty. Kids in my generation heard that from their mothers fairly often.) The same applies to the husband. He "fathers" with primary consideration of the bond between himself and his wife. As these two people rear their children, they are primarily focused on each other.

For a family to work according to God's design, the husband-wife relationship must be far more active than either parent's relationship with any child. Husband and wife must be more involved with each other than either of them is with the children. Their lives must be centered on the bond of their marriage, not the children.

People sometimes ask me, "Won't the children feel left out?" to which I answer, "Yes, and what a blessing that is!"

After all, nothing makes a child feel more insecure than the feeling that his parents' marriage is tenuous, that it could fly apart at any second. It follows that nothing makes a child feel more secure than feeling his or her parents' marriage is rock-solid. So husband and wife give their children one of the greatest of gifts by creating a family in which children are "left out" of the husband-wife relationship; a family in which the children are most definitely not "members of the wedding." That requires that husband and wife create and enforce a boundary around their marriage, one that the children learn to respect. That means, for one thing, that the kids do not share the marital bed, even as infants. It means parents go out on frequent dates without the children. I even recommend that if suitable child care can be found (grandparents, perhaps?), the married couple take one or two vacations a year that do not include the kids. The bottom line is that husband and wife should spend a good amount of time together, on a regular basis, without their children. The family that does "everything" together is not a family operating according to God's instructions.

It goes without saying that when child rearing is done from

within the marriage, it will be done more effectively. Two heads are always better than one. It also goes without saying that when the children do not occupy the center of attention, they will be more independent and will therefore attract less attention to themselves. Therefore, marriage-centeredness makes for a more peaceful home in which children are usually found occupying themselves quietly and the overall level of stress is considerably lower. Last, but certainly not least, paying attention to children demands energy, but when two spouses are paying attention to each other, energy is created! All of this adds up to a much more enjoyable child-rearing experience!

'Til Children Do Us Part

Unfortunately, as the results of my seminar exercise indicate, the above description is the exception, not the rule. In most two-parent families today, one finds that the roles of husband and wife have been displaced by the roles of father and mother. In their parenting, they are focused not on each other, but on their children, who therefore occupy center stage in the family.

Instead of being of "one flesh" with each other, instead of putting their relationship center stage and keeping it there, they are preoccupied with the stuff of child centeredness: They pay more attention to their children than they do to each other, they do more things for and with their children than they do for and with each other, they give more of their time to their children than they do to each other, they talk more to their children than they do to each other, they are more concerned with their relationships with their children than they are with their relationship with each other, they plan their vacations with primary consideration of entertaining the children instead of refreshing their marriage, and so on. When today's all-too-typical dad comes home from work, he comes home to a woman who cannot get children off her mind, and he comes home to play with his kids. It's as if they both took a secret vow on their wedding day that said, "I take you to be my husband/wife until children do us part."

The consequences of this inside-out, upside-down, and turned around backward family situation include:

- *The children lack a model of what being truly married is all about.* Therefore, when they grow up, they are likely to either avoid getting married (which more and more young people are doing)—running instead from one "fly by night" relationship to another—or enter into marriages for all the wrong reasons (e.g., sex, status, financial security, to legitimize children), in which case their marriages are likely to fail.

- *The children develop a sense of entitlement* as regards the disproportionate amount of attention and material things they receive from their parents. They become ever more demanding, disrespectful, petulant, and even outraged at the notion that they should actually lift a finger around the house. As adults, they are likely to bring this same expectation into relationships. Symptomatic of this is the self-centered answer many newly divorced young people give when asked what caused the divorce: "He/she wasn't meeting *my* needs."

- Because the parents are more concerned with having a relationship with than providing leadership to their children, *the children do not receive adequate discipline.* Behavioral problems develop, almost always involving one or more of the "three Big Ds": disobedience, disruptiveness, and disrespect. Quite often, however, these parents have their heads so buried in the sands of a fourth "D"—denial—that they do not even see that their children are undisciplined. They think they're "just being children" while other adults generally think they're obnoxious.

- *When the normal time for emancipation rolls around, the children do not have permission to leave home.* Quite simply, a child cannot emancipate him- or herself easily from the center of the family universe. The center is too cozy. Who would want to leave? Besides, the child in this situation knows that for as long as he can remember, he has been the glue holding his parents together (in psychological terms, this is called codependency). If he leaves, he knows they are likely to divorce.

Indeed, these days, married couples are at greatest risk for divorce shortly after the last child is emancipated. As we all know, many married couples with children never even make it that far. The reasons are many, but surely one big reason is that the people in question stopped being married, really, shortly after they began having children. One flesh became two fleshes. The legal divorce only formalizes what has, in fact, been the case for some time. Isn't this sad? And it's so unnecessary! In most cases, these are people who could have made a go of it if they had simply put God's plan for families, and therefore child rearing, foremost in their minds.

THE POWER OF PREFIXES

I'm often asked how Genesis 2:24 applies to stepfamilies and blended families. Do different rules apply to different family types? No, they do not, and the current notion to the contrary is yet another example of the confusion wrought by the Tower of Parent-Babble. A family is a family. Stepfamilies and blended families are families first, step and blended second. In both cases, therefore, the husband-wife relationship should trump the relationship either parent has with his or her child or children. In addition, stepparents should have blanket permission to exercise complete, unrestrained authority over their stepchildren. A family's prefix should not determine how it should be run.

Unfortunately, most mental health professionals, including the influential Dr. Phil, give exactly the opposite advice. In *Family First,*[2] Dr. Phil says that in step and blended families, the biological parent should discipline only his or her children. This is the worst of the generally bad family advice the telegenic doctor has ever given (and it is the norm in the mental health community). First, it divides the house into two parent-child camps. Second, it marginalizes the stepparent and prevents the marriage from being the relationship of primacy. Downright awful professional advice of this sort is behind a disturbing statistic: *Second marriages involving already existing children are more likely to fail than first marriages.*

More problematic, perhaps, is how Genesis 2:24 applies to parents who began raising children within marriages but are now single because of divorce or death. Being single and being of one flesh with a mate are obviously mutually exclusive. On the other hand (and I most definitely do not mean to twist Scripture here), where one unmarried parent is concerned, *one* can be regarded as either one-half of two or a whole number, as broken or unbroken. The unbroken single parent is a person who regards him- or herself as a fully whole human being and functions as such—a person who lives the fullest life possible. Therefore, I propose the following: *Single parents must make sure they do not get so wrapped up in their kids that they lose their identities and fail to meet their own needs.* In their families, single parents don't have the option of being able to take off their parent hats and put on their spouse hats, so they need to find lives of their own outside their homes, outside being parents. They need to strike a balance between parent and person. A simple principle of parenting physics, one that applies to married as well as single parents, is *you can't give to someone else what you have not secured for yourself.*

I speak with some authority on this subject. My mother was single for most of the first seven years of my life, during which time she did me the greatest of services by not overfocusing on me. She held a job, went to college, and enjoyed a full, rich social life in which I did not participate (other than on very special occasions). She was an unbroken single parent, and it was obvious to me that she occupied a space much larger than "John's mother." Although she had a life separate and apart from me, I never felt the least bit shorted when it came to her love. I always knew that she had more space in her heart for me than for anyone else and that when I needed her she would be there. But I also knew I did not have some exclusive claim on her. She was her own person. Her unbroken independence gave me permission to develop my own interests, learn my own lessons, and carve my own path through life (however meandering it has been at times)—a wonderful gift, indeed.

Unfortunately, many if not most single parents—*especially those who tend to read parenting books*—do not give themselves permission to pursue interests and relationships that do not include their children. So they end up including their children in nearly everything they do, which means they end up doing very little for themselves, which means child rearing becomes far more consuming than it ought to be. The child-centered single-parent home is no more functional than a child-centered two-parent home.

CODA

In November 2006, after I spoke to a Sunday school class in Atlanta, a fellow introduced himself and told me he was a manager in a Fortune 500 company. At recent executive meetings, he said, a major topic of discussion centered on how to deal with parents of young employees who were calling their children's supervisors to complain about bad performance reviews. These are young people in their mid to late twenties, mind you. This parental interference is happening with such frequency that the corporation's lawyers had drafted very specific guidelines that supervisors were to follow in dealing with these parents. He shook his head and said grimly, "We've been having lots and lots of problems with young employees, John. Now we're having problems with their parents."

I have a theory. These are parents who were of "one flesh" with their children for the entirety of their child-rearing years. As a result, they have forgotten how to be of "one flesh" with each other. Another way of saying the same thing: They don't know how to stop being parents. Being parents gives meaning to their lives. If they have to stop, meaning will drain out of their lives and they will have to confront the brokenness in their marriages. To avoid that unpleasantness, they seize upon every opportunity to do what they have learned to do best: protect, enable, and defend their kids.

This does not bode well for America's future, to say the least.

Questions for Group Discussion or Personal Reflection

1. Do the exercise described earlier in the chapter: Of the time you spent with your family during the past week, what percentage was spent in the role of father or mother versus the percentage you spent in the role of husband or wife?

2. Assuming that the past week was typical, is your family child centered or marriage centered? If the former, what can you and your spouse do, *beginning today,* to recenter your family on your marriage? What are you currently doing for your children that you can stop doing without detriment to them (not to say that they may not like that you stop)? What are you currently not doing for each other and with each other that you can begin doing?

3. Imagine a household that isn't child centered. Write down five things that you would be doing differently. What is stopping you from doing those things?

4. What can you begin doing, today, to describe a boundary around your marriage? Is one or more of your children sleeping with you? Are you reluctant to do things without them? Do you plan vacations with them foremost in mind?

5. Are you parenting as one flesh—from within your marriage—or are you parenting as two fleshes? If the

latter, what cultural and social forces have influenced you in that regard?

6. If yours is a stepfamily or a blended family, have you been acting as if the prefix in question should determine how your family operates? If so, what can and should you begin doing, today, to put family truly first?

7. If you are a single parent, have you become so consumed with child-rearing responsibilities that your own needs have been neglected? List five things you can begin doing, today, to take better care of yourself.

CHAPTER SIX

Character First

These commandments that I give you today are to be
upon your hearts. Impress them on your children. Talk
about them when you sit at home and when you walk
along the road, when you lie down and when you get up.
—DEUTERONOMY 6:6–7

Deuteronomy 6:6–7 is the first of God's instructions to parents. It informed Grandma's primary focus, which was to do all she could to see to it that her children became "people of character."

To have God's commandments "upon your heart" means that as a parent you are to live your life according to the model laid out in the Bible, thus being a living example to your children of what is always and forever right and proper. Your example is to be a constant, consistent presence in their lives. The Bible says that you should take every possible opportunity to talk to your children about the difference between right and wrong and guide them toward doing what is right according to the commandments, directions, and instructions God has given us. You should explain to them why you are doing what you are doing, and in your explanation you should always be able to refer to God's Word, the gold standard.

THINK ABOUT IT!

In this key passage, God is also telling parents to discipline their children's thoughts! That's important, because today's parents think discipline is all about behavior. That is, in fact, the logical conclusion that follows upon postmodern psychological parent-babble. Psychology would have parents believe that discipline is all about *behavior* modification—"shaping" proper behavior by manipulating reward and punishment. The Bible, on the other hand, clearly says that discipline is accomplished primarily through proper instruction, by instilling proper *habits of thinking* into one's child. The Bible says that proper thought must precede proper behavior. Jesus says the same thing when he says that before there is adultery, there is lust—in broader terms, before there is sin, there is the thought of sin.

> *You have heard that it was said, "Do not commit adultery."*
> *But I tell you that anyone who looks at a woman lustfully*
> *has already committed adultery with her in his heart.*
> —MATTHEW 5:27–28

It is possible for a person to behave properly without thinking properly. But such behavior is manipulative, de facto, and manipulative behavior—even when it *looks* right—is not respectful. It is by definition pragmatic, self-serving, and clever. Could the fact that so many of today's parents are getting it backward, that they are putting the cart of proper behavior before the horse of proper thinking (it's probably more accurate to say they are trying to move the cart without a horse), explain why so many of today's kids seem so adept at manipulating adults—at doing the right thing for the sole purpose of getting what they want? The question, of course, is rhetorical.

My observation, moreover, is that today's adults are actually reluctant to discipline a child's thoughts—specifically, to tell a child, kindly but straightforwardly, that something he or she has said is simply wrong. I think this has to do with three factors: (a) the general relativism of these postmodern times, (b) the insidious idea that it's not caring for an adult to make a child "feel bad" about something he or she has just said (lower his or her self-esteem), and (c) the wrong-headed and even dangerous notion that a child's mistaken ideas are innocent and do not need to be corrected, that the child will eventually come to right conclusions without adult intervention.

In many of today's schools, for example, teachers no longer mark wrong answers, the theory being that no answer is actually wrong as long as the child in question was making a legitimate effort to solve the problem. It's further believed that marking an answer as wrong could cause a child to develop a negative attitude toward learning. This very dangerous relativistic philosophy has infected the mind-set of many a parent, the result being that many children are being allowed to think whatever they want to think, and pretty much say whatever comes into their minds.

Grandma understood that Proverbs 22:15—"Folly is bound up in the heart of a child, but the rod of discipline will drive it far from him"—is not just a statement; it is also an instruction. It says, "Parents! It is your responsibility to bring the power of your discipline to bear on your child's thoughts!" As in Deuteronomy 6:6 and Matthew 5:28, whenever the Bible says that something is on or in someone's *heart*, the reference is to thought. Today's parents are being lulled into believing that a child's thoughts are innocent, naive, unwitting, unintentional, and so forth, when in fact many of a child's thoughts are the precursors to sin. To not correct them when the opportunity presents itself is sin itself.

MARY, MARY, QUITE CONTRARY

Children express their rebellious natures not only by misbehaving, but by saying deliberately contrary things and challenging statements made by their parents. A fairly frequent parental complaint involves a child who contradicts just about anything his parents say. When they say the weather is nice, the child will insist that it's not; when they say the grass is green, the child will insist that it's red; and so on. Parents ask me if this is misbehavior. Of course it's misbehavior! It is the child asserting that he is his own authority and that his authority is final. Those two ideas are at the core of all misbehavior. It is the child asserting that he has a right, given to him by himself, to think and say whatever he wants to think and say. This is every bit as rebellious as a child refusing to pick up his toys when he is told or a teenager defying curfew. It demands discipline.

"What sort of discipline?" a parent might ask.

That would depend on the age of the child, but this sort of

behavior should be nipped in the bud as soon as it shows itself. To mix my metaphors, this particular snowball rolls downhill very fast. It needs to be stopped before it's completed more than a couple of revolutions. If the offender is three years old, which is when this form of oppositional behavior often rears its ugly head, the parent should immediately sit the child in a "thinking chair" situated in some relatively isolated place for five minutes. When the time is up, the parent should ask, "What color is the grass?" If the child continues to insist that it was red, the parent should say, "Call me when it's green," and walk away. I've heard of three-year-olds who sat for several hours before finally admitting that the grass was green. Such is the power of a child's rebellious spirit!

If the contrarian child is old enough to write, the parent should sit him at the kitchen table, give him paper and pencil, and tell him that he can get up when he has written "The grass is green" one hundred times in neat script. Above all else, it is essential that the parent not argue with a child over issues of this sort. The moment a child denies the truth of something obvious a parent has said, the parent should calmly enforce his or her authority. Argument only confers status on the child's assertion that he can think as he pleases. A child indulged in this fantasy is a child headed down the perilous path of postmodern relativism.

> *I need no warrant for being and no word of sanction upon my being. I am the warrant and the sanction.*
> —AYN RAND, ANTHEM

GET A GRIP

The discipline of character also requires that parents discipline a child's emotional expressions. The necessity of this was once, and not so long ago, understood implicitly, but then along came psychologists in the 1960s who said that children should be allowed to express emotions freely; that forcing them to "bottle up" their feelings (as traditional parents had done) would cause various adult neuroses.

This psychological bogeyman was cut from whole cloth, just like all the rest. However bogus, the propaganda was successful, which is why it is no longer unusual for five-year-olds to still be throwing wild tantrums when they don't get their way. The melodramatics characteristic of today's teens, especially female, is yet another indication that parents no longer feel they have the right to tell children that beyond the third birthday, tantrums, sulking, and petulance are not allowed and will be punished.

But it doesn't begin and end with tantrums, sulking, and petulance. A child who cries when crying is not appropriate should be taken aside and told, firmly, to get control. A child who laughs inappropriately should be removed from the situation, read the proverbial riot act, and made to apologize to those present. Yes, even a three-year-old.

"Oh come on!" a well-meaning parent might well be exclaiming. "Three-year-olds can't be expected to know when some impulsive reaction is inappropriate!"

A three-year-old who does not know that a certain impulsive reaction is inappropriate should be taught, as forcefully as necessary, that the reaction is inappropriate. Indeed, today's parents have difficulty with this because Postmodern Psychological Parenting has caused adults to lower their expectations of children. Fifty years ago, the idea that a three-year-old should be reprimanded for laughing inappropriately would not have caused anyone second thought; today, many people think it borders on child abuse. They would say the child couldn't help it, to which I would say, "Then someone needs to help him develop the necessary self-restraint so that next time, he'll be able to 'help it.'" The lower our expectations concerning children, the more we tolerate behavior that should not be tolerated, and the more undisciplined children will become.

WHO'S ON FIRST?

God is also telling parents, in Deuteronomy, that they should be the *number-one influence* in their children's lives, and not just when their children are young, but through the teen years. Parents cannot "impress" themselves and their values upon children under any other circumstances. Unfortunately, in today's world, parents are often not the number-one influence in their children's lives. Too many parents allow other influences—their children's peers, teachers, coaches, television, music, video games, the Internet, and so on—to take precedence over their own. Here's how easily this can happen.

Billy the Kid

For the purpose of illustration, let's say that Billy, age ten, goes to bed at nine and wakes at seven, on average. Over the course of a year, therefore, Billy is awake for 5,110 hours, during which he spends 1,260 hours in school and on the way to and from school. That leaves 3,850 hours. He spends an average of four hours a week going to and from and participating in after-school activities, for a total of 208 hours, leaving 3,642 hours. The typical ten-year-old spends twenty hours a week watching television, so if we assume that Billy is typical, he's watching 1,040 hours of television a year, leaving 2,602 hours. He spends 360 hours on homework and school projects, leaving 2,242 hours. He plays video games an average of one hour a day—365 hours in a year—leaving 1,877 hours. He plays with his friends an average of an hour a day, so that leaves 1,512 hours. He is allowed on the Internet an average of one hour a day, leaving 1,147 hours. He spends an hour a day playing with his toys, working on hobbies, or just doing nothing, leaving 782 hours. He is in a church youth group that meets two hours a week, leaving 678 hours—the time his parents have to be of influence. Unfortunately, they're doing other things at least half of that time, so the actual influence they have over Billy is 339 hours a year. If time translates to influence, Billy's parents are exerting less influence over him than his teachers, peers, television, coaches, video games, and the Internet. The family is not Billy's primary environment, and his parents are not his primary influence. If the truth were known, it's been this way in Billy's life since early on, because both of his parents work outside the home. Before he was in school, he was in day care and pre-school.

Family situations that fit the above description are all too common today. Parents, usually without realizing it, decrease as influences in their children's lives as other things increase in influence. In some cases, the other influences eventually lay a claim on the child; they take over the child's life in very undesirable ways. A true story will serve to illustrate what I mean.

The Virtual Teenager

In the fall of 2006, a mother wrote me through my website, asking for advice concerning her fifteen-year-old son. The boy had become obsessed with playing Internet games. I must admit to not knowing exactly how such things work, but apparently "gamers"—usually teens and young adults with too much time on their hands—from all over the world congregate on certain websites to play various virtual reality games. The mother told me that she and her husband had "limited" their son's play to six hours a day, six days a week. If they tried to persuade, much less force, him to stop playing electronic diversions and interact with the family, he would go ballistic—screaming, cursing, throwing things, and the like. The parents were at a loss as to what to do.

I told them they were describing an addict, and that their son's addiction to virtual reality games was every bit as debilitating as a drug addiction, the only difference being that his drug was electronic, not chemical.[1] I told the parents that the next day, after he left for school, they should remove the computer from his room and put it in storage away from the house. I emphasized that "cold turkey" was the only effective way to break the hold of an addiction. Making him cut back on his gaming time, even assuming that was possible, wasn't going to work.

Two weeks later, I received my next email from the boy's mom. She told me that she and her husband had done what I recommended, and sure enough, their son had gone not simply ballistic, but supercalifragilisticexpialidocious-ballistic. He had pounded on furniture, threatened them with physical harm, and threatened to run away, all the while cursing nonstop at the top of his lungs. When he realized that wasn't going to work, he had withdrawn to his room and demanded to be left alone.

Within a few days, however, he had come out of his room and was beginning to interact, however tentatively, with the rest of the family. He began doing chores around the house, even things he hadn't been asked to do. Best of all, he told his parents that he hadn't liked what they had done, but he now felt "relieved." He actually thanked them! The mother described him as much more relaxed, communicative, helpful, polite, and happy. He was smiling a lot more. She said, "I feel like I have my son back."

That may be a "tip of the iceberg" story, but the boy's addiction to electronics is hardly an anomaly in this day and time. The story illustrates how quickly and quietly parental influence can slip away and be replaced by something that may look harmless at first, but is quite the opposite. It's a story that also reflects how generally insecure today's parents feel concerning their authority. But it's also a hopeful story—it demonstrates that when parents wake up and determine to retake the position of being the number-one influence in a child's life, no matter how far down the road to ruin the child may have gone, it is possible to regain that status. Make no mistake about it, however, situations that far gone require drastic measures.

Are you the number-one influence in your child's life? Here's an exercise I put parental groups through, which I invite you to do as well:

1. Make a list of the influences in your child's life—television, popular music, the Internet, movies, after-

school activities, coaches, video games, books, school, teachers, peers, and so on.

2. Using time spent as the primary criterion, rank those influences from most influential to least influential.

3. If you and your family aren't at the top of the list— the number-one influence in your child's life—make a second list of things you need to do in order to reclaim that important role.

4. Beside each item on that second list, write the *exact date* you intend to implement that action, and make yourself a promise that you won't allow anything in the world to interfere.

Have you allowed television to eclipse your influence in your child's life? Are you willing to remove your child's television from his room? Are you willing to make yourself more available to your child by significantly cutting back on your own television watching? Are you willing to do that beginning today?

Do after-school activities demand so much time that the family rarely spends time together? (Remember, watching television "together" is not a family activity, nor is cheering from the sidelines while a child plays soccer.) Are you willing to pull your child out of after-school activities—or at least cut back significantly on the time they consume—and use that time to go on family picnics, to museums, to historic sites, and even on simple walks in the park? If the answer is yes, then my next question is "When?" After all, time's a'wastin'!

A FINAL WORD ON SELF-ESTEEM

I cannot emphasize enough that according to both the Bible and good research, possessing high self-esteem and being a person of character are incompatible. When it comes to persuading parents that the quest for this particular grail on behalf of one's children is a misadventure, the problem is that over the past four decades high self-esteem has become as American as apple pie. For someone to say "high self-esteem is a bad thing" is akin, therefore, to saying apple pie is poisonous. Incredulity is the common reaction.

One very typical rejoinder: "But I want my child to possess a lot of self-confidence! Don't self-confidence and self-esteem go hand in hand?"

No, they don't. For one thing, there is no evidence that when modesty and humility were cultural standards, the America people suffered lack of confidence. The history of America, from the Pilgrims through World War II, is anything but a history of quitters. Besides, high self-confidence is fine as long as it's tempered by realistic self-assessment. Without the latter, self-confidence often translates into recklessness. In that regard, the research finds that people with high self-esteem tend to think they are capable of excelling at anything and everything. This is the sort of pride that goes before a fall. In overestimating their aptitudes, people with high self-esteem tend to be boastful and take foolish, often life-threatening, risks. They drive too fast, try something they've seen an extreme-sports athlete do on television, think they are impervious to the toxic effects of alcohol, and so on. That describes all too many of today's teens. It's worth saying at this point that adolescence and delusions of immortality do not, as commonly believed, go hand in hand. Many of today's teens have no appreciation for their mortality, it's true, but teenagers in prior historical eras were not described as reckless and foolhardy. Those characteristics are symptoms of high self-esteem, which was lacking in teens until fairly recently. The bottom line: Humility governs self-confidence; without humility, self-confidence is potentially hazardous to self and others.

Sometimes a parent will ask, "But certainly you don't believe in low self-esteem, do you?"

In this case, the opposite of high is not low. The opposite of high self-esteem is humility, modesty, and "meekness" (strength under control). That is the biblical ideal, and granted, it is an ideal. Sin is all about self-esteem, and human beings are sinful; therefore, the ideal of having *no* self-esteem will forever remain an ideal. Nonetheless, we can and should aspire to it. That's not the least bit contradictory. To take another example: A person cannot *become* Christ, but he or she can aspire to *be like* Christ. That's a good thing, right? Likewise, aspiring to a state of no self-esteem is a good thing. Did Jesus esteem himself? No, he most certainly did not. Jesus was the only individual who has ever lived who had no self-esteem. We can't be him, but we can sure emulate his example.

Plain and Simple

The Amish aspire to no self-esteem. They even have a term for outbursts of self-esteem: prideful. When a member of an Amish community lets fly with an outburst of self-esteem (for example, he acts opinionated), another member of the community will gently rebuke him by saying, "That's prideful" or something similar. When an Amish person is so rebuked, he doesn't become defensive. Quite the contrary, he expresses thanks to the person who restored his humility, who helped him get his feet back on the ground.

The Amish aspire to a Christ-like state of no self-esteem, yet they are some of the most resourceful and emotionally healthy people in the United States, perhaps the world. Studies of the Amish find that they suffer mental health problems at roughly half the rate of the rest of the population. Furthermore, pediatricians who treat Amish children find little if any incidence of attention deficit disorder, oppositional defiant disorder, or any of the other behavior disorders currently plaguing children who live in what the Amish refer to as "the world." An Indiana pediatrician with whom I've communicated services eight hundred Amish families. The average number of children born to an Amish couple is seven. Assuming that many of the families in this pediatric practice have yet to reach full size, let's just say, for sake of discussion, that the average number of children per family in his practice is three. That's twenty-four hundred children, of which "not a single child in this group has been referred to us by the schools for evaluation or recognized by us as having ADD." Raising seven children, Amish parents experience far fewer problems in the area of discipline than average American parents experience raising only two. Obviously, the Amish are doing something right. I suggest that what they're doing is as simple as raising children according to God's Word.[2]

Questions for Group Discussion and Personal Reflection

1. Do you think you have been sufficiently attentive to the need to discipline your child's thoughts? Have you at times been reluctant to correct something your child said, some idea he or she expressed, even though it was definitely wrong? If so, do you see how you have been unwittingly influenced by the relativism of the age?

2. List three things you can begin doing, today, to more effectively *impress* the difference between right and wrong (your values) on your children. Here's one to get you started: "I need to take more opportunities to point out to my child when someone does the right thing in an everyday situation."

3. Have you been an unwitting victim of propaganda to the effect that young children should be allowed "freedom of thought" and "freedom of emotional expression"? What does your child do and say that indicates you have been somewhat remiss when it comes to disciplining your child's thoughts and feelings? What can you do to turn that around?

4. Take the exercise on pages 140–141. Are you the number-one influence in your child's life, or have you allowed other influences to eclipse your own? If the latter, what are those influences? What do you need to begin doing, today, to reclaim and occupy the position of number-one influence?

CHAPTER SEVEN

Farsighted Parenting

Train a child in the way he should go, and when he is
old he will not turn from it.
—PROVERBS 22:6

Where there is no vision the people get out of hand.
—PROVERBS 29:18 NJB

If there is one verse of Scripture that more represents God's
design for child rearing than any other, it is Proverbs 22:6.
Of those verses that refer to the upbringing of children, it's also
one of the best known. Its meaning is obvious: Parents should
aim their child rearing at a target that lies some distance off in
the future.

One's aim in this regard should be unwavering. It needs to
be maintained every hour of every day and in every situation.
Furthermore, because the "way" a child should go does not vary
from child to child, every parent should be aiming at the same
target: an adult of right character, morals, and ethics who loves
God. That adult is a responsible and compassionate citizen, a

devoted spouse, and a parent who "passes it on"—a parent who trains up his children in the way they should go. Maintaining that aim requires that a parent hold in the forefront of his "parent mind" a clear vision of the kind of person he wants his child to be when his child is thirty years old—a vision to which he regularly refers.

Ask yourself, "Do I have such a vision, and if so, do I hold it in the forefront of my mind?"

AIM AT THE GOAL

Unfortunately, most parents today—if they were being truthful—would have to answer no and no again. Did you? If so, you're hardly alone. With rare exception, today's parents are nearsighted. They are not aiming their parenting at a clear vision of their children's futures. Instead of parenting with the long-range goal in mind of responsible adults, people in secure possession of good character, and the like, all too many of today's parents are focused on short-range goals that lie no more than several months to a year down the road. Not surprisingly, given the importance today's parents tend to attach to their children's skills, the short-range goals in question are usually academic in nature—helping their children make perfect scores on weekly spelling tests, helping them make good grades on their next report cards so as to advance their chances of being accepted into gifted and talented programs, enrolling their children in numerous after-school activities so as to increase their extracurricular aptitudes, and so on.

Parents who start out being nearsighted, furthermore, nearly always remain nearsighted. They move from one relatively immediate goal to another, then another, and so on. It's also the case that nearsighted parents usually pour enough energy into any given short-range project to all but ensure its accomplishment. The resulting gratification creates the illusion that they are on a proper course, when, in fact, they have no real sense of direction at all. Their myopic zeal, and the short-term satisfaction that results, blinds them to the fact that they are not training up their child in the "way he should go." They are all but completely out of touch with any vision of their child's future, his adulthood.

At this very moment, for example, the well-intentioned parents of some three- year-old, somewhere, are focused on doing all they can to make sure he learns the alphabet and basic number facts before his next birthday so as to increase his chance of being admitted, next year, to the most exclusive private school prekindergarten program in town. Once he learns his letters and numbers, they will hire a tutor to teach him to read, their goal then being that he will enter "real" kindergarten reading at a second-grade level, at which point their goal will become persuading the school's headmaster to let him skip first grade. When that is accomplished, they will focus their energies on seeing to it that he is accepted into the gifted-and-talented program and then into a magnet school for science and math. To accomplish that, of course, means that he will have to make good grades, so his parents will help him with his homework (every night), help him with his projects (every one), help him review for tests (every one), and so on and so forth. Indeed, his elementary school transcript will be nearly perfect—a redundancy of As.

What's wrong with that? one might ask, to which the answer is nothing, as far as it goes. Unfortunately, that's as far as it goes.

Does making straight As "train up a child in the way he should go"? No, it does not. As do I, every reader knows of someone he went to school with who was an exemplary student but who made a mess of his or her life as an adult.

If I asked the parents of this three-year-old to describe the person they want their son to be when he is thirty years old, they would not say anything remotely akin to "We want him to be a member of MENSA, celebrated as one of the most intelligent people in the country; we want him to have already risen to national prominence in his field, to be married to the daughter of the wealthiest couple in town, to be living in a five-thousand-square-foot mansion in a gated country-club community, to be the envy of all who meet him and a close friend of and confidant to influential politicians."

Instead, they would almost surely say something along these lines (and let us assume that these parents are devoted Christians): "We want him to be a responsible, charitable, honest, reliable, and compassionate citizen, a devoted family man, and to possess a steadfast love of the Lord."

In short, they would not describe their future thirty-year-old in terms of his prestige, accomplishments, or material wealth. They would describe him in terms of his *character*. But it is quite obvious that their day-to-day parenting is not focused on training up an adult of character; it is focused instead on training up an adult of prestige, power, and position. It is focused, in other words, on superficial characteristics rather than matters of *substance*. Furthermore, these parents fail to realize that many of the day-to-day things on which they are spending their parenting energies are actually counterproductive to raising the adult they would say they want to raise.

.. questioned at length and in detail, these parents would no doubt say they want their child, as a thirty-year-old adult, to be a self-starter, a person of initiative. Yet their day-to-day efforts are clearly teaching their child to depend on their initiative, to stand not on his own two feet, but on theirs. They would probably say they want their son, as an adult, to understand that failure is often necessary to eventual success, and to be motivated rather than discouraged by it. Yet their day-to-day efforts are preventing him from experiencing failure! How is he to develop a positive attitude in the face of disappointment if his parents protect him from any and all forms of it?

When I talk about Proverbs 22:6, I often begin by asking parents in the audience to write down their long-range goals for their children. Inevitably, one or more parents will write "college-educated." That's fine as far as goes, but planning for college is not the sort of future vision I'm talking about. Nor is it the sort of long-range goal referred to in Proverbs 22:6. I'm referring, and so is the Scripture, to the adult *person,* not that person's accomplishments. The *way* referred to in Proverbs 22:6 has nothing to do with worldly achievement—academic, financial, professional, or otherwise. It refers to the child's *walk* in life, the manner in which he conducts himself, especially when the chips are down.

One's life walk is a matter of *values,* not accomplishments; of *character,* not worldly goods. Besides, good character is not prerequisite to obtaining a college degree. Nor is good character obtained in college, as evidenced by the fact that a fair number of people with college degrees are found to possess major character flaws. The same could be said about becoming a medical doctor, a famous actor, a celebrity athlete, or even the president of the United States.

Furthermore, when I ask parents who've just told me they want their child to go to college, "Would you rather that your child obtain a degree from a prestigious university but be untrustworthy, deceitful, and/or sexually promiscuous as an adult or that he *not* go to college but be an adult of impeccable character?" they always choose the latter, and without hesitation. But are these same parents aiming their present parenting at that thirty-year-old adult of impeccable character? No, they're pouring most of their energy into ensuring that their child makes good grades *on his next report card* in order to advance the goal of going to a prestigious university and eventually becoming a person of prestige and power.

Nearsighted parenting is synonymous with parenting that is often frantic and, therefore, exhausting. That's because nearsighted parents are micromanagers. Not *some* of them, mind you, but *all* of them, and micromanagers are always frantic and exhausted. Parents who are in constant short-term mode tend to zigzag all over the parenting "map" like a ship without a compass. This makes the raising of a child far more arduous, far more stressful than it otherwise would be, no matter how inherently "difficult" one's child may be.

The Shortest Distance Between Two Points

By contrast, parents who stay focused on a long-range child-rearing vision are able to move themselves and their child steadily and in a more-or-less "straight line" from early childhood to adulthood with the least amount of effort, using the least amount of energy. In making any parenting decision, they give primary consideration to the long-range vision—the *person* they want their child to be when he is thirty or so years old—rather than some arbitrary short-range goal. Their day-to-day parenting decisions, therefore, "match" the long-term vision and steadily advance them toward it.

Parents who fit this description experience the raising of children as being relatively easy and almost always rewarding. Oh, they will have their share of difficulties along the way. All parents do. Human nature makes inevitable that any child will give his or her parents a certain amount of trouble. But for parents of this description, child rearing is not difficult and arduous in and of itself. After all, they are parenting according to God's clear instruction that we should train up children in accord with the way they should go as adults, and when one goes about any task according to God's instruction, accomplishing the task will be relatively simple, though not always easy and painless. However, with his instruction comes God's enablement and empowerment to do what he's called us to do. He hasn't made parenting complicated—we have! And the less one adheres to God's design in some area of life, the more complicated and difficult that part of life will be.

Come to me, all you who are weary and burdened, and I will give you rest.
—MATTHEW 11:28

Furthermore, because farsighted parents are focusing on long-range rather than short-range goals, they don't sweat small, day-to-day details. For this reason, their parenting is relaxed and their feathers are rarely ruffled. By contrast, parents who are nearsighted, who focus on one short-term goal after another, cannot help but sweat the small stuff. They micromanage, and micromanagers, in whatever context they are found, are always in a near-constant state of busyness. Short-term goals tend to pile up on one another—finish one and there's another one waiting for you; finish that one and there are two more waiting for you; finish those and there are three more waiting for you; and so on. Needless to say, micromanagers are not only constantly busy to the point of frenetic, they are also tense, anxious, and uptight. Micromanagers also fail to see that they are their own worst enemy, that their own approach to the task is the problem. Not realizing this, they blame the people they manage for their perpetual stress.

Likewise, the micromanaging, short-term-oriented parent frequently complains about how her children stress her out, how they are "difficult," how they never give her a moment's peace, and the like. She doesn't realize that the problem is not her children—it's her.

McPARENTING AND THE APOCALYPSE

"No parenting decision is difficult to make," I tell my audiences, "if you *tune* the decision to that long-term vision of the adult you are raising. That approach will keep you moving steadily and in a more-or-less direct path toward that goal. When you find yourself especially troubled by a certain child-rearing situation, confused about what decision to make, take a deep breath and focus on that vision. Your confusion will clear, and the right decision will become apparent."

Making the Grade

Concerning any child-rearing issue, nearsightedness results in one parenting behavior while farsightedness results in quite another. Take the issue of homework, for example. Out of a desire to help their children get good grades—a short-range goal—a good number of today's parents help their children with their homework nearly every school night. When they describe these "help" sessions to me, they do not describe relaxed, enjoyable occasions. Rather, they talk about how frustrating these sessions often are, for both them and their children. Finishing homework seems to take twice as long as it should, they say. They keep on having to reteach the same things, over and over and over again. As soon as they begin the homework marathon, their otherwise gifted children start acting dumb as rocks.

If I ask one of these parents, "Is that the way you want to spend your evenings?" she (more than 90 percent of the parents in question are female) will not hesitate to tell me, emphatically, "No, that is definitely *not* the way I would prefer to spend my evenings."

But will she stop micromanaging her child where homework is concerned? Not likely, because like all micromanagers, the homework micromanager is convinced that if she doesn't help her child do his homework, or at the very least hover over him while he does it, making sure he does it right, either (a) it won't get done or (b) it won't get done right. Those are unacceptable outcomes to this nearsighted parent. In her mind, the fact that when she orchestrates a homework session the homework gets done and done right means she is doing the right thing. That's because people who are short-term oriented are also easily misled by short-term gratification. They seem to think that if what they're doing—micromanaging—yields desirable results, they should keep right on doing what they're doing. This is an example of what I call "McParenting." Just like fast food, Mc-Parenting has no value beyond that of satisfying an immediate need or reaching some short-range goal; furthermore, habitual McParenting, like eating all of one's meals at fast food joints, will lead to major problems down the road.

The fact that these parents are focused on the short-range goal of making sure that their children make good grades (if the truth were known, the parents are making the grades, not the kids) drives them to do what they clearly don't enjoy doing. Furthermore, all of this "helping" obviously isn't resulting in children who take responsibility for their homework and do it independently. Yet if you ask these parents, "What's more important to you: that you grow a child who is a responsible and self-starting adult, irrespective of the grades he received in school, or that you grow a child whose grades in school were always good (because you made sure of that), but who, as an adult, tends to be intimidated by challenge and has difficulty with initiative?" they will always say they would prefer the former. When pressed, they are able to admit that responsibility, resourcefulness, and initiative are infinitely more important to ultimate success in life (not the sort of success measured by prestige or material wealth, but the success of living one's life in accord with God's design) than good grades, yet they will still come up with all manner of justifications for continuing to help their children with homework. In other words, they recognize that the long-range goal outweighs the short-range goal, and they even will admit that their myopic habits may well be getting in the way of more important long-range objectives, but they cannot bring themselves to act accordingly.

The Sky Is Falling

McParenting goes hand in glove with "apocalyptic thinking"—imagining that if you don't properly attend to some small parenting problem, today, right now, this very minute, it will rapidly spiral out of control and eventually ruin your child's chances for success in life. You think, for example, if you don't make sure that every one of your child's homework assignments is turned in sans flaw, he'll fall further and further behind in school, drop out of high school, never go to college, fail at one menial job after another, and at age thirty be found pushing a grocery cart filled with all of his possessions through the streets of some major city during the day and sleeping at night in a cardboard box underneath an overpass. Apocalyptic thinking exaggerates the negative to absurd degree.

Staying with the subject of homework (because it happens to be where a disproportionate amount of McParenting is taking place these days), not one parent has ever told me that when she stopped micromanaging her child's homework and handed over the responsibility to him, the child crashed and burned academically and never recovered. Yes, things got worse in the short run. After all, when something is propped up artificially, there is bound to be some degree of collapse when the supports are removed. In every single case, however, the "suffering" has been temporary. The child's grades slip for one, maybe two, report-card periods (in most cases, however, the slippage takes place for no more than several weeks). Then he begins to learn how to stand on his own two feet and experience the intrinsic reward of doing so. Eventually, these kids do better in school than when their parents were helping them, and that includes kids with learning disabilities! After all, the old adage does say "Things get worse . . . *before they get better.*"

Parents guided by a long-range vision of the adults they are trying to raise hold their children all but completely responsible for doing their own homework and doing it properly. Accordingly, they place conservative limits on the amount of homework help they are willing to dispense on any given evening (for example, they will give five minutes of assistance on each of two homework problems on any given school night). Consistent with their overall disdain of micromanagement, they rarely even ask their children if they have homework. Because it is clear that responsibility for their homework belongs all but exclusively to them, these children do their homework, do it properly, and turn it in on time. (For more specifics on this sort of approach to homework, the reader is referred to *Ending the Homework Hassle,* Andrews McMeel, 1991.)

Amy's Anguish

I am reminded of a situation that developed concerning my daughter, Amy, when she first encountered the mental rigors of high school geometry. The first homework assignment of the year completely threw her, and she came to me, tearfully, for help.

"Daddy," she said, choking back sobs, "I just don't understand this! It doesn't make any sense to me!"

I consoled her, sat her down at the dining room table, and spent upward of an hour explaining the logic of geometry to her. Finally, she experienced a "breakthrough" and was able to complete the assignment. She kissed me and virtually danced back up the stairs to her room. Needless to say, I was brimming with fatherly satisfaction.

The next night, at about the same time, she appeared before me again, choking back sobs. "I just don't understand geometry, Daddy," she cried. "I think I should drop the course!"

I counseled her to not rush to judgment, and once again we sat together at the dining room table until she got it and I got my kiss and she went dancing up the stairs. The next night, she again came to me for help, again sobbing. And the next, and the next, and the next, and. . . . Finally, I got it. My help was ensuring that Amy would get good grades on her geometry homework and maybe even her geometry tests, but it was also ensuring that she would forever and always feel intimidated by anything geometrical and perhaps even any mathematical operation more complicated than simple division.

So, some two weeks into this dance, Amy appeared one evening, at the appointed time, sobbing. She couldn't understand geometry. She didn't understand the assignment. She needed my help.

"No, you don't need my help, Amy," I said. "You *think* you need my help, and the more I help, the more you think you need my help. So, I've decided I'm not going to give you any more help with geometry. I think I've helped you get off to a fairly good start in geometry. From this point on, it's up to you."

She gave me the most incredulous of looks. She asked if I was kidding. No, I wasn't. Did I realize, she said, that if I didn't help her with geometry, she was going to fail geometry, and perhaps not be able to get into a good college?

Apocalypse! I had to remind myself that although a young lady, she was still a child, and that children are prone to dramatic thinking, especially when they think life has overwhelmed them. (Proverbs 22:15 [NLT] says, "A youngster's heart is filled with foolishness.")

"No, Amy," I said, calmly, "you are not going to fail geometry. You're going to do fine, actually. I know you, and I know you'll work on geometry until you get it."

"No! You *have* to help me! I don't understand this! If you don't help me, I'll fail geometry!" And the tears flowed copiously.

"I'm not going to help you any more, Amy," I calmly said. "And that's that."

Her eyes narrowed. She glared at me as no female has ever glared at me. Finally, she said, "Fine, then! I'll just fail!" And she stormed off, stomping up the stairs.

Amy made an A in geometry that grading period. She made an A the next grading period, and the next, and the next. If I had helped her, would she have made As? Perhaps, but she would not have advanced an inch toward the vision I had of her as an adult, a vision of a competent, capable, and confident woman.

Hands Off

Willie and I learned all of this the hard way, courtesy of our own kids, beginning with our son, Eric. In January of his third-grade year, Eric's teacher told us that she was not going to promote him to the fourth grade. He was at least a year behind in his skills. In addition, he was exhibiting all of the symptoms of both attention deficit disorder and a learning disability.

To that point in time, Willie and I had orchestrated nightly homework marathons to assure that he did his homework and did it correctly. A few days after that January meeting, we told Eric that we were no longer going to make sure he did his homework. We weren't going to explain things to him, help him with his assignments, or even ask him if he had homework. We told him he was on his own, that if he passed the third grade it would be on his own merits, not ours.

"But how am I going to pass without your help?" he fretted.

"Eric," I said, "if we have to help you get to the fourth grade, then your teacher is right—you shouldn't be there."

Three months later, in April, his teacher told us she felt as if she'd witnessed a miracle. Eric was reading at grade level, doing grade-level work, and all of his behavior problems had cleared up as well. He went to the fourth grade with the rest of his classmates and by the end of that year was making straight As. Eric learned valuable lessons from this experience, but so did Willie and I. He learned how to stand on his own two feet. We learned how to let him.

A few years later, when Amy was in the fifth grade, she came to me one evening in a panic. She'd forgotten that her first-ever science project was due the next day. I had to take her to the store and buy the materials she needed and help her put it together. I refused. She insisted. I refused. She collapsed in tears. I must hate her, she wailed. She'd surely fail science, and it would be my entire fault. I stood firm. Ultimately, she did her project without help from either Willie or me, turned it in a week late, received a fairly bad grade, and never again forgot to properly prepare for a test or project.

THE AFTER-SCHOOL FRENZY

Another thing most of today's parents can be found doing, day in and day out, is driving their children from one after-school activity to another, from soccer to art lessons to piano lessons to martial arts instruction to social dance lessons to youth choir practice to scout meetings to—you get the picture, I'm sure. You may even fit that description yourself! It is not at all unusual, these days, to encounter a parent who will admit, proudly, that she drives each of her three children to two after-school activities a week, every week of the school year. That's six activities a week, some forty weeks a year, for a grand total of 240 round trips!

Not surprisingly, these parents often complain about how worn out they are from driving their children from one activity, event, or lesson to another. It never seems to occur to them that these activities are arbitrary, optional. They always seem to have what sounds like good reasons for doing all of this hustling.

Whose Team Are You On?

"I want my son to learn how to be a team player," said a father whose ten-year-old son plays at least one after-school sport a season—sports that he will not be playing when he is thirty years old—in addition to at least two other after-school activities at any given point in time. This father also does not realize that the very best of all contexts in which to learn to be a team player is within one's own family, by doing chores, by obeying the rules, by carrying out instructions properly, by sharing with siblings, and so on.

Unfortunately, the child who is being driven from one after-school activity after another, who is at football practice until nine on two school nights a week, twelve to fifteen weeks a year, is learning more about how to be a good *football* team player than he is learning how to be a good *family* team player. Pray tell, which learning will prove more valuable to this child when he is thirty? Needless to say . . . And another needless to say, this family and everyone in it would be a lot more relaxed if each of the kids was allowed only one after-school activity per season, to a grand total of three per child per year, with the caveat that no activity could keep the child out past seven in the evening or interfere with the family meal, which will occur at a reasonable hour and at home.

Does football train up this child in the way he should go? No it does not. That training can only be properly done within what I call the "classroom of the family." For being focused on short- instead of long-range goals, these parents lose sight of the big picture and wind up being often harried, exhausted, and with nothing to show for it but a child who has learned how to play team football. It's forgone, when parents focus on short-range goals, that their priorities—priorities they will acknowledge when questioned—get completely out of whack.

Girls Just Wanna Have Fun

When Amy was in what today is equivalent to middle school and junior high school, she experienced painful social difficulties. They were painful for her, and they were painful for Willie and me as well. Amy was small for her age, and her physical development lagged behind that of most of the other girls in her class. When she was thirteen, she looked like she was ten, maybe eleven. Boys paid her no attention (for which we were thankful), and she wasn't really interested in boys (thankful squared). It was, therefore, difficult for Amy to relate to girls who were "boy crazy," and they didn't want her hanging around either. She was excluded from all of the cliques, so when she complained to us that she had no friends, she was telling the truth.

Willie and I wanted desperately to solve this problem for her. We thought of calling some of the mothers of the more popular girls and asking them to help us. We thought of throwing a big expensive birthday party for Amy and inviting all of the popular girls. The more we thought of ways we could help solve the problem for Amy, the more anxious we became concerning Amy's popularity and the more angry we became toward the popular girls and their parents. It became difficult for us to sleep at night.

We finally came to our senses. We could not solve this problem for Amy. Furthermore, any attempts on our part to solve it might well make the situation worse. Oh, the popular girls might come to her birthday party just to ride the Arabian stallions we'd imported from Spain, but that wouldn't make them any more inclined to invite Amy into their cliques. Amy would wind up feeling even more rejected than she already felt. We shifted our focus from the short-term goal of helping Amy elevate her junior high popularity quotient to the long-term goal of raising an adult who did not depend on other people's approval in order to feel that her life was in order.

From that point on, whenever Amy complained about having no friends, or that other girls didn't like her, Willie and I would say something along these lines: "Amy, we know this is painful, but you will not be thirteen forever. Someday, you will be thirty, and all this will seem unimportant then. Furthermore, what you are experiencing today is helping you learn how important it is to never treat another person the way these girls are treating you. It's also helping you learn to stand on your own two feet, to not depend on other people for a sense of well-being."

She did not like that at all. When we responded to her pathos in that fashion, she'd gather herself up in an indignant snit and stomp off, making it clear to us that she did not appreciate our point of view. Sometimes, she'd even start crying pathetically, sobbing as if her life was at an end. It was all we could do not to start planning that big party.

When Amy was in high school, she found a friend. And then another. And then another. By the time she graduated and went off to college, she had lots of friends, many of whom she keeps up with to this day.

One day, when Amy was in her midtwenties, she and I were reminiscing about her childhood. She brought up the social difficulties she experienced in early adolescence, and she said, "You know, Daddy, I hated it when you and Mom would tell me that my social problems were going to help me be a stronger person, but now I am that person, and I realize the wisdom of what you were trying to tell me."

Eyes on the Prize

No matter the parenting problem or issue, there are two perspectives: short-term and long-term. Acting solely on the basis of the short-term perspective may solve the immediate problem, but it rarely advances the child toward the long-term vision. Acting with the long-term vision uppermost in mind may result in short-term pain, but it nearly always results in long-term gain.

This is not to say that there aren't certain situations in which parenting decisions and actions should be determined by short-term goals. Those situations are usually readily apparent, however. They are often of an "emergency" nature. For example, if your child is seriously ill, there's nothing to be gained by taking a "wait and see" attitude because you want your child to learn to be stoic about such things. You need to get your child to a doctor. If you discover that your teenager is using drugs, you need to act, and act now. Sometimes, the short-term goal and the long-term goal are one and the same: for example, making sure that your child makes it to age thirty. But again, those situations are not the norm. They are the exception, and the sort of parent who is found reading this book will need no help distinguishing them.

The operative question: Is your parenting behavior consistent with how you want your child to "go"? Is it in accord with Proverbs 22:6?

When asked, "Do you want your child, when he is thirty, to be a materialist? Do you want him to believe that the acquisition of material things is essential to a sense of well-being, of personal satisfaction?" parents will always answer no, absolutely not. But do these same parents buy their children much, if not most, of what they want? Do they make sure, to the best of their abilities, that their children do not lack what most of their friends have in the way of material possessions? When their children are upset about something, do they often buy them things to cheer them up? Unfortunately, the same parents who answer no to the first question will answer yes to the next three. They have good intentions, to be sure, but they do not have a long-range vision that they "aim" their parenting at on a daily basis. They do not realize that in child rearing, one can win the day-to-day battles and yet still lose the war.

As an elderly woman once remarked to me, "Today's parents have lost sight of the prize."

Have you?

Questions for Group Discussion or Personal Reflection

1. When making day-to-day parenting decisions, do you frequently "check in" with a vision of the adult you want your child to be when he or she is thirty years old? Are you generally nearsighted or farsighted as a parent? If the former, give several specific, recent examples of how certain parenting decisions would be different if you were more focused on long-range goals.

2. Write down ten adjectives that you hope will describe the adult you want your child to be when he or she is thirty years old. Then ask yourself if your day-to-day parenting efforts and energies are properly aimed at producing an adult that fits that description. Are you, like most parents, more concerned with short-term objectives that have little if anything to do with the person of character you really want to raise? If so, what do you need to change about your parenting in order to bring it into accord with Proverbs 22:6?

3. On a scale of one to ten, rate your day-to-day parenting in terms of how frantic and stressed-out it is. If the rating is higher than five, how much of the stress can be attributed to energy spent accomplishing short-term objectives that are of questionable long-term value?

4. On a scale of one to ten, rate your parents' day-to-day parenting in terms of how frantic and stressed it

was. Were your parents less focused on short-term objectives? Did they often just let the proverbial cards of child rearing fall where they may? Are you less willing to do that? If so, why?

5. Has a concern with accomplishing short-term objectives pushed you in the direction of micromanagement? If so, how, specifically, are you micromanaging? Thinking in terms of just one area in which you are micromanaging, what do you think the short—versus long-term consequences would be if you completely stopped?

6. Think of several ways that you are or have been guilty of McParenting (and, most likely, apocalyptic thinking). Homework, perhaps? Concerning each of those issues or problems, what is or should have been the farsighted approach? If you adopt the farsighted approach and things get worse, do you think they will eventually get better? Is your parenting apocalypse as near as you imagine it to be? Is it real at all?

CHAPTER EIGHT

To Everything,
Turn, Turn, Turn . . .

There is a time for everything,
and a season to every activity under heaven.
—ECCLESIASTES 3:1

L ike farming, raising livestock, gathering maple syrup, and the migrations of fish and birds, the raising of children is marked by seasons. These seasons were established by God; therefore, they cannot be altered at the whim of man.

Each of them is defined chronologically, and just as each of Earth's seasons requires of a farmer a unique set of tasks, so each of parenting's seasons requires a specific parental role and distinct parental responsibilities. A farmer who conforms his behavior to the unique characteristics of each of agriculture's seasons is all but assured a high yield.

Likewise, parents who conform their behavior to the unique requirements of each of the seasons of child rearing will be all but assured a "high yield" of reward and satisfaction out of seeing their children advance toward and eventually claim responsible maturity.

THE SEASON OF SERVICE

The first of these, the Season of Service, begins at birth and lasts approximately two years. During this initial season parents function as servants to a child who cannot serve himself and cannot anticipate the consequences of his actions. His dependency and ignorance (not to be confused with lack of intelligence!) require that his parents place him at the center of their attention and orbit around him in a near-constant ministry of surveillance and "doing"—checking, feeding, carrying, changing, comforting, fixing, fetching, and so on.

The purposes of season one are threefold:

- To "root" the child securely in the world—to assure him that he is where he belongs, with people who love him and who will take good and proper care of him under any and all circumstances.

- To provide for the child's fundamental biological needs—put bluntly, to keep him alive and thriving.

- To prevent, as much as is humanly possible, the child from hurting himself.

In all cultures and in all times, the mother has been and is the primary servant during season one. (There have been and are exceptions, but they are individual exceptions that have not significantly tilted the historical norm.) The father, even one who wants to be highly involved, stands slightly outside the periphery of his wife's busy orbiting. He is her "parenting aide." Like a teacher's aide's, the husband's job is to assist his wife and fill in for her when she needs a break. Consequent to this child centeredness, the marriage is "catch-as-catch-can" during season one. (To those of you who have noticed what may appear to be an inconsistency between what I say here and what I have earlier said about mothers orbiting around their children and fathers playing the role of "parenting aide," I will simply say [paraphrasing Ecclesiastes 3:1], "There is a time for everything . . . but it is not the entire time.")

Now, an infant or young toddler may not yet have well-developed language skills, but he is highly intelligent nonetheless. He is drawing inarticulate conclusions concerning the workings of things in his microcosm (which is the one-and-only world as far as he is concerned), one of which is that his mother is there to do his bidding and that he has power and authority over her. He verifies this by crying, at which his mother appears and does everything in her power to fix whatever it is that is causing his distress.

Grandma understood that whereas her ministry was a necessary one, she was slowly creating a monster. If she did not bring this first season to a close, she was in danger of raising a spoiled brat—a child who would believe that as his mother was continuing to do, so the world revolved around him. She realized that out of absolute necessity she had caused her child to believe that he had power over her, that she was his gofer; therefore, she had to step up to the plate and correct that impression. And so, around her child's second birthday, as he became more capable of doing basic things for himself, Grandma began to make the critical transition from the first of parenting's seasons to its second. Under normal circumstances, this transition takes about a year. It is, without question, the most significant and precedent-setting of all times in the parent-child relationship, the future of which hangs in the balance.

To bring about this transformation, a mother must begin:

- Teaching and expecting her child to do for himself what she has previously done for him—use the toilet instead of diapers, get his own cup of water and basic snacks, dress himself, pick up his toys, and so on.

- Building a boundary between herself and her child, thus limiting his access to her—making him wait before she does something for him, refusing to pick him up (pointing out that she is involved with something else), instructing him to go elsewhere while she finishes a task.

- Backing slowly out of a state of high involvement with her child and re-establishing a state of high involvement with her husband, thus bringing his tenure as parenting aide to a close.

THE SEASON OF LEADERSHIP AND AUTHORITY

As is so often the case when seasons change, this transitional year is marked by storms of protest from a child who wants season one to go on forever. Who can blame him? Who would not want a servant for life? But if the mother stays the course, then by the time her child has reached his third birthday, he will see her with new eyes: once a servant, now a formidable authority figure who is not to be trifled with. Where once he was at the center of her attention, she is now at the center of his. She insists that he do more and more things for himself, that he give her "space" to do what she needs and wants to do (including putting her feet up and doing nothing), and makes it perfectly clear that her relationship with his father trumps her relationship with him. And so begins the Season of Leadership and Authority, during which time the parents' job is to govern the child in such a way that he (1) consents to their government (becomes their willing disciple), and (2) internalizes their discipline and gradually develops the self-restraint necessary to govern himself responsibly.

This is not to say that parents should never serve a child who is in season two. There will, in fact, be times when service is absolutely necessary, but whereas service is the rule in season one, it should be the exception from that time on.

THE SEASON OF MENTORING

Season two lasts for ten years, from three to thirteen, at which point a second transition takes place (or should) that moves parent and child into season three, the Season of Mentoring. It is no coincidence that in traditional cultures, early adolescent rites of passage—Jewish bar and bat mitzvahs being extant examples—occur when a child is thirteen. These rituals mark and celebrate a major transition in the parent-child relationship. They acknowledge that the child in question has completed the disciplinary "curriculum" of season two and is now regarded as self-governing. He no longer needs adults to tell him what and what not to do; rather, he needs adult mentors to help him acquire the practical skills he will need to emancipate successfully—how to apply for a job, balance a budget, plan for the future, and the like.

THE SEASON OF FRIENDSHIP

The successful emancipation of the child marks the end of season three, the last season of active parenting, and the beginning of season four, the Season of Friendship. During this last and most rewarding of parenting's seasons, the child's parents are parents in the biological sense only; in reality, parents and child now regard one another as peers. The younger peer may seek guidance from one or both of the older peers, but that is no different from one friend seeking the counsel of another. In season three, guidance was provided largely at the parents' initiative; now, guidance is provided largely at the initiative of the biological child.

Within the framework of this seasonal approach to parenting, children emancipate relatively early. In Shakespeare's time, males were fully emancipated by age eighteen. As recently as 1970, the average age of successful emancipation was twenty. Today, the average age of successful emancipation is approaching twenty-seven, and many young people—so-called "boomerang children"—make several vain attempts before finally succeeding. In the four hundred years between Shakespeare and 1970, the average age of male emancipation increased two years. In the next thirty-seven years, that average increased by nearly seven years. Something is obviously wrong.

Season	Age of Child	Parent Role	Parenting Goal
Service	Birth–2	Servant	Secure child
Leadership	3–13	Authority	Self-governing child
Mentoring	13–18/21	Mentor	Emancipated child
Friendship	Emancipation	Friend, counsel	*Good* friend to child

SEASONAL BREAKDOWN

These days, child rearing is rarely taking place in accord with its natural seasons, and it has not been since the 1960s. The universal symptoms, in reverse order: boomerang children and increasingly late emancipation; disrespectful, self-destructive, depressed, irresponsible teenagers; and toddler characteristics (short attention span, impulsivity, low tolerance for frustration, inability to delay gratification, tantrums, defiance, and so on) exhibited well beyond chronological toddlerhood.

The breakdown is occurring between the second and third birthdays, when it is imperative that a mother initiate the transition between season one and season two, then team with her husband and complete it. She must (1) shed the role of servant (for the most part) and step into the role of authority figure, disciplinarian, and leader of the child, and (2) bring her husband out of the role of parenting aide and effectively "remarry" him. This transition took place rather smoothly and reliably fifty and more years ago; it takes place rarely today. Grandma had unmitigated permission from the culture and all the support she needed to bring about this sea change in her child's life. Today's mother lacks both permission and support.

The New Good Mother

The new standard to which all too many of today's mothers conform has it that the Good Mother:

- Serves not for two years or so, but in perpetuity—that as her child grows, she finds more and more ways of being involved, of demonstrating her abiding commitment to him.

- Always has her child at the center of her attention and uppermost in mind even when she isn't with him.

- Is highly involved with her child in nearly every area of his life.

In short, today's typical mother bends unwittingly to cultural pressure and becomes "stuck" in season one. She becomes, for all intents and purposes, married to her child. It is as if she took the following vow on her wedding day: "I take you to be my husband until children do us part." Because she regards service to her child as the be-all and end-all of good mothering, she is incapacitated in her ability to assume leadership of and authority over her child.

The principles of leadership are the same from one leadership context to another. The same attributes that make for a good corporate CEO make for a good military leader. In whatever arena they are found, effective leaders are able to

- Make unpopular decisions and stay the course.

- Delegate responsibility so as to challenge the capabilities of those they lead.

- Establish a boundary between themselves and those they lead.

Those same attributes also make for a good leader of children. If he or she does not abide by the above principles, a corporate CEO will fail in his or her responsibility to convey authority effectively, and so it is with a parent. Unfortunately, the new standard of good mothering paralyzes a mother's ability to make decisions that cause her child distress. A servant, after all, is supposed to please and be pleasing. If today's mother makes a decision that upsets her child, she is likely to interpret her child's angst as an indication that she has made the wrong decision and reverse her course.

The new standard virtually requires a mother to be a micromanager, perpetually scurrying from one task to another making sure everything is going as it should. Once upon a time not so long ago, children worked for their mothers. By the time a child was three years old, his mother had assigned him to household chores. By the time he was four, he was doing nearly as much for his mother as his mother was doing for him. By the time he was five or six, he was doing more. Today's mother believes that the more a mother does on behalf of her child, regardless of the child's age, the better mother she is. So, even today's typical seven-year-old child is virtually chore-free. His mother even helps him with his homework every night (a new criterion of good mothering).

The new standard denies a mother permission to establish a boundary between herself and her child. It says that the Good Mother is highly involved with her child, and the more highly involved, the better. Under the circumstances, it is verboten for today's mom to ever, under any circumstances, deny her child access to her. If he wants her attention, she is to drop what she is doing and give it. She is even to sleep with her child if he demands it!

My mother, typically of her generation, had no problem shooing me out from underfoot, even telling me I had no permission to be in the same room with her if she was doing something that required her undivided attention. At those times, she would usually warn me that if I didn't find something to do and leave her alone, she would find something for me to do. In that regard, my mom was typical of her generation. Today's mom is horrified at the mere thought of telling her child that something she is doing is more important than something he wants her to do.

I remember my mother saying to me, "John Rosemond, you don't need a mother right now, and I'm not going to be one." She said it calmly and matter-of-factly; therefore, I knew she was serious. When I share that with people my age (I was born in 1947), they recall something similar their mothers said to them.

It is the rare mother today who can bring herself to say something equivalent to "you don't need a mother right now, and I'm not going to be one." The psychobabblers have convinced her that speech of that sort will cause her child psychological disruption, generate an "attachment disorder" or "bonding issues," cause him to question her love for him, send his self-esteem into a tailspin, or all of the above. They have successfully implanted in her head a swarm of "psychological bogeymen" that cause her to be constantly afraid that one wrong step in her parenting will shatter her child's supposedly fragile psyche.

Under the circumstances, it is impossible for today's typical mom to assert a calm, matter-of-fact authority. She is caught in a conundrum: On the one hand, she is expected to be highly involved with her child; on the other, she is expected to discipline him properly. These two expectations cancel each other. As a consequence, today's mother is frustrated in her attempts to discipline. She experiences more discipline problems than her grandmother even thought possible. Thus the great paradox of modern parenting: women have claimed authority in the military, education, the professions, the workplace, and the church and yet abandoned their authority where their children are concerned. The woman of fifty years ago did not have the extra-familial opportunities available to today's woman, but she exerted a powerful authority over her kids. I submit that today's children are not developing respect for female authority, and that this is going to come back to haunt us all in the very near future.

FOOD FOR THOUGHT

After giving a talk in Charlotte, as I was exiting the auditorium, I was stopped by an older woman who said, "Now I get it, John!" She told me that her thirty-something daughter, a feminist and single mother, occupied the highest position in her corporation ever held by a woman. "Now I understand," she said, "why she has no problem exercising authority over adults through the day, but then goes home and takes orders from my four-year-old grandson."

The problem is compounded by the fact that the Good Mother's husband can't move beyond his season-one role either.

His wife (in reality, she is his ex-wife) orbits around their child well past the time when that orbiting should have drawn to a close. She becomes stuck in the role of servant to child, so he becomes stuck in the role of parenting aide. He is likely to compensate for the loss of relationship with his wife by striving to enter into close relationship with his child; thus, the new ideal in American fatherhood is to be *best buddy* to one's child.

Attention Deficit Family Disorder

And so it is the case that many a child today is being raised by a servant and a buddy. Needless to say, those circumstances are not conducive to successful discipline, the key to which is simply that parents have a child's attention. Just as a child who is paying attention to his teachers can be taught without great effort on their part, a child who is paying attention to his parents can be disciplined without great effort. But the following is axiomatic: *The more attention parents pay to a child, the less attention the child will pay to them.* Period!

By age three, a child has come to one of two conclusions concerning his relationship with his parents:

Conclusion one: It's my job to pay attention to my parents.

Conclusion two: It's my parents' job to pay attention to me.

A three-year-old who reaches conclusion one can be successfully and fairly easily disciplined. He has figured out that it is his job to pay attention to his parents. They have caused him to figure this out by moving out of season one and into season two. They are no longer a servant and a parenting aide; they are a husband-and-wife team of authority and leadership. Because they command his attention, they rarely if ever have to demand it. And because they have his attention, he obeys. It's as simple as that.

On the other hand, a three-year-old who is still convinced it is his parents' job to pay attention to him cannot be successfully disciplined. Let me repeat that for emphasis: *cannot be.* The child who reaches conclusion two has acquired, by age three, an attention deficit. Not attention deficit disorder, mind you, because there's nothing at all wrong with him. Nonetheless, there will definitely be disorder in the house. His parents will say things like, "He doesn't listen to us," "We have to yell to get his attention," and "We have to repeat ourselves several times and then get right up in his face before he does what we're telling him to do." Yep, he has an attention deficit all right, but not one caused by a chemical imbalance or some malfunction in his brain. This attention deficit was caused by well-meaning parents who think that the more attention one pays one's child, the better parent one is.

Unfortunately, most three-year-olds today have no reason to arrive at conclusion one. More unfortunately, children still have no reason to do so when they are four, five, six, seven, nine, or twelve. So, today's typical parents come to the threshold of season three having not completed the curriculum of season two. They have not governed, they have served and "buddied"; therefore, their child has not learned the fundamentals of successful self-government. He has little respect for authority because one does not learn respect for authority from a servant and a buddy. He has not developed the ability to delay gratification, deny himself, tolerate frustration, or stand on principle, all of which are necessary to effective self-government.

Thus deficient, he enters his teen years, and having never developed any loyalty to his parents' values, he begins to sway to and fro in the breezes of peer group pressure, the foremost dictum of which is that it is not "cool" to acknowledge the legitimacy of any adult authority. So this already wayward thirteen-year-old is belligerently disrespectful toward his parents, refuses to obey their rules, begins hanging with the wrong crowd, and so on. His parents' anxiety level—mixed with equal parts anger, resentment, and guilt—begins to climb. They begin to imagine the worst—drugs, delinquency, dropping out—none of which is outside the realm of possibility, in fact.

After attempting to negotiate and compromise (to no avail, because if you give a terrorist an inch, he will take a mile) and talking themselves blue in the face, their almost inevitable response to this burgeoning rebellion is to try to impose discipline that probably would have worked in season two on a season three child. The problem is that season two discipline is fairly specific to season two. It does not work well, if at all, in season three. The mismatch kicks the child's rebellion into high gear, and the parents wind up with all-out warfare on their hands.

I've heard this story over and over and over again. In fact, there is not one reader of this book who does not know parents who are in the very situation described above. Such is the price we are paying for believing that because people have capital letters after their names they know what they are talking about.

"You Never Had a Curfew?"

When my late father was in his early eighties, I asked him, "Dad, when you were thirteen, what was your curfew?"

"I never had a curfew, son," he replied.

"You could stay out as late as you wanted?" I asked, incredulous.

"No, son," he said. "I never stayed out as late as I wanted. I knew when to be in."

"Well, Dad, if you knew when to be in, then you had a curfew. That's what I'm asking here. What was it?"

"I know what you're asking, son," he said, a bit irritated now. "I may be old, but I'm not senile. I told you, I never had a curfew."

"Then how'd you know when to be in?"

"Son," he said, slightly exasperated that his own progeny could not figure out something so elementary, "by the time you're thirteen, you'd have to be a fool not to know when to be in."

I have spoken to other people, male and female, of Dad's generation about the issue of curfew, and most of them have told me that when they were youngsters, they did not have curfews either; like Dad, they knew when to be in. By age thirteen, they had successfully completed the curriculum of season two courtesy of parents who had functioned as leaders of children during that time. Their "curfews," which they set for themselves, were based not on their own self-interest, but on respect for their parents. They were self-governing—but do not confuse self-government with self-determination.

Self-determination is self-idolatry. It is the belief that you, the almighty individual, know what is best for you, and that you have the right to make whatever choices you want to make. Adam and Eve, with a little help from the serpent, decided they were self-determining. Today, belief in the legitimacy of self-determination is growing, as reflected in the ubiquitous use of the phrase "your truth." Self-government, on the other hand, rests on a solid foundation of respect for others and especially respect for legitimate authority. Valid self-government cannot take place without submission to that authority, submission to what is right.

That's what we've lost by subscribing to Postmodern Psychological Parenting: children who submit willingly to legitimate authority, who do the right thing because it's the right thing to do. That's the bad news. The good news is we can get it back together, but climbing uphill takes a lot more energy than sliding down. Are you willing to do the work?

Questions for Group Discussion or Personal Reflection

1. On a sheet of paper, draw four columns and label them (1) Child, (2) Age, (3) Proper Season, (4) Actual Season. Then fill in that information for each of your children. Are you in the season you should be in with each child? Or have you become "stuck" in season one with one or more of them?

2. If you are stuck in season one with one or more of your children (children who have reached their third birthday), take a second sheet of paper and describe what that state of "stuckness" looks like. What are you doing for your children that they are capable of doing for themselves? How are you acting more like a servant than either an authority figure or a mentor?

3. If you are stuck in season one with one or more of your children, what specific things can and should you do to unstick yourself? How do you think your children will react to this revolution in their lives? Will it matter to you if they do not like it? If so, why?

4. What social pressures caused you to become stuck in the first place? To some degree is peer approval dependent on your continuing to function as if all of your kids were season-one children? Is that what all, or nearly all, of your peers are doing? Are you willing to step out of the "parenting parade" and become your own person? What might be the social conse-

quences to you of doing so? Are you willing to shoulder, endure, and prevail against those consequences?

5. At what age were you emancipated? At what age would you ideally like your children to be emancipated? Is each of them presently on track to accomplish that? If not, what do you need to do to get that process back on track?

6. Is there a clear boundary, which you enforce, between yourself and each of your season-two or -three children? If not, what problem behavior can be attributed to that lack of boundary? What specific things do you need to do to begin erecting that boundary, starting today?

7. Has each of your season two children reached conclusion one or conclusion two? If the latter, what do you need to begin doing to correct their attention deficit, beginning today?

8. Are you willing to start the revolution *today*? If not, what are your excuses?

PART THREE

Discipline

Discipline is the biggest of all bugaboos for today's parents, the reason being they believe in behavior modification. They believe in *methods,* but the problem is their point of view, something no method will correct. Furthermore, no method will work for long in the absence of the right point of view. On the other hand, just about any method will work for a parent with the right point of view. The one and only right point of view is the biblical one. Just as the Bible tells us what children are like, it tells us how to discipline them properly. Not surprisingly, the Bible says nothing about behavior modification.

CHAPTER NINE

The Bible Tells Me So

Trust in the LORD with all your heart and lean not on
your own understanding.
—PROVERBS 3:5

The Bible has a number of very pertinent things to say and
instructions to give concerning the discipline of children.
The importance of proper discipline stems from—as the Bible
tells us—the innate sinfulness of children. Children do not have
to be taught to misbehave; misbehavior comes naturally to
them. In any given situation, a child is inclined, by human
nature, to do the wrong thing, not the right thing; the self-
serving thing, not the other-serving thing. The positive influence of significant adults who are committed to the goal of
raising a person of character is essential if a child is going to
make, and keep making, the choice to behave properly, in a
manner that is both respectful to others and respectful to self.
The following ten scriptural principles, amplified by the verses
that support them, are essential to understanding the importance of proper discipline to a child's upbringing.

1. DISCIPLINE AND LOVE ARE TWO SIDES OF THE SAME COIN

The LORD disciplines those he loves, as a father the son he delights in (Proverbs 3:12).

In the 1970s, I was the first parenting pundit to assert that a family should be operated as a benevolent dictatorship. It was my intention to convey that proper parenting was constituted of equal measures of powerful love and powerful leadership. The Latin root of benevolent means "for the good of," and the root of dictator is dictate, which simply means to tell with authority. I felt the term captured the essence of good parenting rather nicely. I quickly discovered, however, that many people, especially professionals who taught and worked with children, only heard "dictatorship." The resulting knee-jerk reaction was usually accompanied with lots of shouting and general boorishness. In my vain attempts to defend and explain myself, I came to realize that these same people thought love was enough to raise a functional child. No matter what word I might have used to reflect authoritative leadership, the idealists would have suffered convulsions.

It's all well and good for someone to say he *loves* someone else, but that profession of love is meaningless without affirming action. In the case of parental love, proper discipline is one such affirmation. The Bible says that discipline is an expression of delight in one's child. The more parents delight, the more effectively they discipline, and the more effectively they discipline, the more they will delight. The Bible also says that parents who discipline their children properly are doing the Lord's work. It should go without saying that more gratifying employment cannot be found.

2. PUNISHMENT IS NEVER PLEASANT BUT PRODUCES GREAT BENEFIT FOR THE PERSON PUNISHED

No discipline seems pleasant at the time, but painful. Later on, however, it produces a harvest of righteousness and peace for those who have been trained by it (Hebrews 12:11).

When the writer of Hebrews pointed out that no discipline seems pleasant at the time, he was referring to corrective discipline, and he was essentially saying that if correction is not painful to the person corrected, it will have no effect.

Two generations ago, parents had no problem making children feel bad when they did bad things. Postmodern Psychological Parenting, with its emphasis on the need to protect self-esteem, has resulted in a parental conundrum: parents who (1) attempt to correct their children's misbehavior while (2) taking great care not to make their children feel bad. The two efforts cancel each other. As a consequence, the antisocial behavior of children continues unfettered (and worsens over time), parents become ever more frustrated in their attempts to discipline, and mental health professionals enjoy higher standards of living.

3. PUNISHMENT IS ESSENTIAL TO PROPER DISCIPLINE

Because the Lord disciplines those he loves, and he punishes everyone he accepts as a son (Hebrews 12:6).

In the mid-1970s, I took a course to become certified as a "Positive Parenting" instructor. At the time, our first child was seven and I was just beginning to come to grips with the fact that most of what I had been taught in graduate school was useless.

After two days in this week-long course, I realized that the "discipline" being taught wasn't discipline at all. It was talking, reasoning, and explaining. I asked the psychologist who was teaching the course why the word *punishment* was conspicuously lacking in his lectures and the course materials. He answered that punishment lowered self-esteem and caused behavioral problems to become worse. "It's just not a loving way to correct misbehavior," he said. Well, the Bible says proper discipline, including punishment when appropriate, is an expression of love. Who are you going to believe?

4. PROPER DISCIPLINE VALIDATES A CHILD

If you are not disciplined . . . then you are illegitimate children and not true sons (Hebrews 12:8).

What's this? If a child is not disciplined, the child is not legitimate? That's pretty heavy stuff. It's the equivalent of saying that parental failure to discipline is a form of child neglect. In this day and time, the courts sometimes terminate the parental rights of people who are found to have neglected their children. In effect, the writer of Hebrews was saying what courts recognize—that parents who neglect their children in whatever fashion are not valid. They fail, furthermore, to validate their children. As a mature individual is justified (validated) to God by his or her faith, a child is justified to society (turned into a functional citizen) through proper parental discipline.

5. OBEDIENT CHILDREN ARE PLEASING TO THEIR PARENTS

Discipline your son, and he will give you peace; he will bring delight to your soul (Proverbs 29:17).

Everyone knows parents whose children are disobedient, sassy, and so on. Do they seem to be at peace? Do they seem to delight in their children? Of course both questions are rhetorical. Parents who are content with and in their parenting have children who are respectful, well-mannered, and obedient. The opposite is true as well: It never fails that parents who seem constantly under stress, exasperated, and worried have children who are ill-behaved. Such parents are convinced that their children's ill behavior is the cause of their stress, but that belief is a form of denial. The real problem is the lack of proper parental discipline. The Bible is clear that in order for a child to bring a parent peace rather than discord, the child must be properly disciplined. In other words, whether a child brings a parent peace or turmoil is up to the parent. It's not a matter of being "lucky," of some roll of cosmic dice that produces, quite by accident, a "good child." That's exactly what some parents believe, but properly behaved children are no accident. They are the product of parental purpose.

6. CHILDREN ARE TO OBEY THEIR PARENTS

Children, obey your parents in everything, for this pleases the Lord (Colossians 3:20).

God wants a relationship with us, but a relationship with

God requires self-discipline. It goes like this: Parents who properly discipline their children are likely to raise self-disciplined children who have what it takes to become permanent citizens of the Kingdom. No wonder the obedient child is pleasing to the Lord. It's the only thing on his wish list!

7. OBEDIENCE WILL BRING BLESSINGS TO CHILDREN

Listen, my son, to your father's instruction and do not forsake your mother's teaching. They will be a garland to grace your head and a chain to adorn your neck (Proverbs 1:8–9).

A parent who says, "I wish my child would obey me!" (and we've all heard parents say it) just doesn't get it. First, children do not grant adult wishes. Second, that parent wants his child to obey for *his* benefit; so that *he* won't be so frustrated and stressed-out all the time; so that *he'll* have more peace of mind. But the Bible clearly says that although parents are certainly blessed by children who are well behaved, the primary blessings of good behavior flow to the children themselves; good manners are like fine jewelry—they grace the person who "wears" them.

8. THE MOST OBEDIENT CHILDREN ARE ALSO THE HAPPIEST, MOST SELF-RESPECTING CHILDREN

He who ignores discipline despises himself, but whoever heeds correction gains understanding (Proverbs 15:32).

The happiest parents always seem to have the most obedient children, and the most obedient children are the happiest children. Happiness abounds for those who are obedient, in large part because obedience to legitimate authority is not only a sign of respect for the person in authority, but also of self-respect.

Disobedient people, wherever they are found, are never found to be happy. They are angry, sullen, malcontents who "despise themselves." Lacking respect for authority, they also lack self-respect.

The connection between obedience and happiness is confirmed by the research of Dr. Diana Baumrind of the University of California. In a thirty-year study of parenting outcomes, Baumrind discovered that children who score highest on adjustment scales tend to have parents who adhere to a traditional model. As regards discipline, these are parents who have no reluctance to punish, even spank, their children for misdeeds (albeit said spankings tend to be occasional and not the rule).

9. A LACK OF DISCIPLINE CONTRIBUTES TO DEATH—IN THE EVERLASTING SENSE

Discipline your son, for in that there is hope; do not be a willing party to his death (Proverbs 19:18).

Hope. No guarantees, just hope. Proper discipline sets a child on the right road, but it's up to him to see to it that he stays there—or finds his way back when he strays. Proper discipline from parents makes it less arduous and painful for a child to properly discipline himself, to stay to the narrow path—the path to life eternal, the opposite of which is death. Parents! Give the gift of hope to your children!

10. DISCIPLINE IS THE WAY TO LIFE ETERNAL

These commands are a lamp, this teaching is a light, and the corrections of discipline are the way to life (Proverbs 6:23).

Jesus made the bold statement that he is the "way and the truth and the life" (John 14:6). Through him, we are granted eternal life. In Proverbs, we are told two things: Discipline is the way to life, and a lack of discipline leads ultimately to death. That's how important discipline is. It makes *all the difference in this world and in the world to come!* Through proper discipline, a parent gives a child the greatest gift of all. Amen!

Questions for Group Discussion and Personal Reflection

1. Are the behavioral expectations you have for your child in keeping with the behavioral expectations your parents had for you at the same age? If not, what are the social and cultural influences that have caused your expectations to be lower?

2. When your child misbehaves, do you tend to hold back on punishment? If so, why? Are you concerned that your child will grow up with negative memories of his or her childhood? Are you worried about lowering your child's self-esteem? Are you afraid your child will interpret punishment to mean you really don't love him? Do you want your child to like you? Were your parents concerned about these sorts of things? Did you always know that your parents loved you? Did you have a happy childhood?

3. Do your children know that God wants them to obey you? Have you read them Colossians 3:20 and Proverbs 1:8 and discussed why obedience is important?

4. Do you often want your children to obey for *your* benefit, so that *your* life will be made easier? If so, how would your discipline change if you always disciplined for *their* benefit, with no thought of yourself?

5. Is your authority a reflection of God's authority? Are you a truly "godly" parent? If your answer to either of those questions is equivocal, what do you need to do to bring your authority over your children into better alignment with God's authority over us all?

CHAPTER TEN

Leadership Discipline

Those who spare the rod of discipline hate
their children. Those who love their children care
enough to discipline them.

—Proverbs 13:24 NLT

With rare exception, today's parents believe in behavior modification—that "correct" consequences, correctly used, will correct a child's misbehavior. In Chapter 2, I explained why behavior modification works with animals, but not with children (or humans of any age, for that matter). The question becomes, What sort of discipline does work with children? Before I answer that all-important question, I'd recommend that you go back and reread that Chapter 2 material, but if you'd rather not, here's a capsule review:

- One of the architects of postmodern psychology, Professor B. F. Skinner, proposed that human beings were subject to the same laws of behavior as were animals (an atheist, Skinner believed humans *were* animals). In the 1960s, the media popularized his theories, and it wasn't long thereafter that people were using the terms "behavior modification" and "discipline" synonymously.

- Behavior modification is what one does to train an animal to either perform a certain task or substitute an acceptable behavior (for example, scratching at the door) for an unacceptable one (urinating on the floor). The aims of behavior modification are achieved by manipulating reward and punishment, and without a doubt, the technique works very well on animals—horses, dogs, rats, pigeons, and even amoebae.

- Evidence that behavior modification works reliably on human beings is lacking. Correct consequences will change the behavior of a dog, but a human child, even a toddler, possesses two attributes that an animal does not possess: free will and a rebellious nature. These unique qualities enable the child to do what an animal cannot do: deny that a consequence, even one that is highly punitive, has any power or relevance in his or her life.

- Consequences, used correctly, *compel* animals to change their behavior. Because they do not possess free will, animals have no choice in the matter; therefore, whether the change in behavior is for the better or worse is up to the animal's handler.

- Consequences cause humans to make *choices,* and the choices are not always for the better. With humans, "correct" consequences can and often do backfire. Sometimes, after experiencing a powerful consequence, a person will become that much more determined to resist any and all attempts to manipulate him. Most parents have seen demonstrations of this attribute in their children's behavior. Where children are concerned, whether a consequence brings about behavior change is not up to the child's "handler"; it's up to the child. A correct consequence may persuade the child to make a correct choice; then again, it may not.

THE (BEHAVIOR) MOD SQUAD

Two friends of mine are certified behavior modification experts. They work with autistic children and are so good at what they do that they have clients all over North America.[1] At this writing, my friends also have a three-year-old. To their befuddlement, behavior modification does not work on their son.

When he misbehaves, they punish him. When he behaves properly, they reward him. He continues to misbehave. Sometimes it seems that he's more likely to continue doing what they punish him for than what they reward him for. My friends also told me that nothing they learned in their graduate programs—stuff that works with autistic children—works with their own child! That's easily explained. In a normal child, free will is the main determinant of behavior. In an autistic child, autism is the main determinant of behavior. When free will is not dominant, or when, as is the case with an animal, it's not part of the organism's makeup, behavior modification works. Autistic children aren't consciously, purposefully rebellious. My friends' three-year-old is a rebel, and he's very conscious of and purposeful about what he's doing. He has decided to show his parents that they have no control over him, that nothing they do to him is going to cause him to submit to their authority. Behavior modification is simply inadequate to deal with the toddler's battle cry: "You're not the boss of me!"

Please do not misunderstand me on this point: It is vital that children understand that different choices result in different consequences. But that understanding does not guarantee proper behavior. Where children are concerned, consequences are merely packets of information. The information contained in any given consequence ought to reflect (albeit "in miniature") how the real world would respond to the same behavior on the part of an adult. Take a child who refuses to obey instruction from his parents. In the real world, if an employee refuses to obey instructions from a superior, the employee will probably find himself out of a job. His standard of living will be suddenly lowered, which means that he will have fewer options.

Parents cannot exile a defiant six-year-old from the house, but they can and should lower the child's "standard of living" and restrict his freedom for a period of time. That could be accomplished by taking away favorite playthings and confining him to his room for several days (meaning any time he's not at school, eating a meal, or using the bathroom). One can only hope that the information contained in these consequences will cause the child to "think twice" the next time his parents give him an instruction, but it may not. Only time will tell.

Rebel with a Cause

So what should parents do when consequences have "failed," when they have done the right thing and their child keeps right on doing the wrong thing? They should keep doing the right thing—they should keep right on delivering consequences. They should never give up the good fight. (I'll deal with this issue in greater detail in the next chapter.) The fact that the child doesn't seem to be learning his lesson doesn't mean that his parents are doing something wrong, that the consequences are wrong, or that the child is suffering from some psychological or organic malfunction that prevents him from learning his lesson. It says only that the child is what I call an "uppercase rebel," as in REBEL.

The misguided belief that right consequences produce right behavior is the source of most of the frustration many of today's parents experience in the area of discipline. It is also a prime source of income for mental health professionals. When a certain consequence or methodology does not bring about a lasting change in a child's behavior, today's parents conclude they are using the wrong approach and begin to search for a consequence or method that will work. They search books, magazines, newspaper articles, and the Internet. They find a reference to a new method in a book. They try it, and it works for a while, and then it stops working. They go looking for a new method, and so on. Almost invariably, the parents end up getting more and more frustrated as they proceed to exhaust their options. Finally, completely at wit's end, they wind up in a psychologist's office.

He listens to their tale of woe and tells them that when a child's behavior is this resistant to behavior modification, it means there is something amiss with the child's biology. He diagnoses attention deficit disorder or oppositional defiant disorder or childhood bipolar disorder or some combination thereof. The psychologist sends a report to a psychiatrist, who sees the child for thirty minutes, concurs with the psychologist, and prescribes a drug. At no point in the diagnostic process was the child given even so much as a cursory physical examination. Nevertheless, the parents believe the psychologist knows what he is talking about when he asserts that the child's behavior problem is rooted in his or her biology—that it arises from a "biochemical imbalance" (brain fluids were not collected and analyzed) or "inadequacies in the left frontal lobe inherited from the father's side of the family" (no brain scan was performed, no genetic testing was done).

Making Disciples

Here's the question no one seems to be asking: If these behavioral problems are inherited, how is it that they were virtually unheard-of fifty-plus years ago? Over the past two generations, there's been a mind-boggling increase in the number of children who come to school with serious behavioral problems, but that's not the half of it.

Today's kids are doing things that people who raised and taught children in the 1950s cannot relate to. For example, every single kindergarten teacher with whom I've spoken in more than five years has reported that she has been recently hit or kicked or had something thrown at her by a five- or six-year-old child. Then there's the related matter of what I term the "hidden domestic abuse epidemic": children who have passed their third birthdays (meaning they are no longer toddlers, chronologically) who are hitting their parents—their mothers, usually—on a regular basis. The list goes on and on and on: eight-year-old children throwing wild tantrums, even in public, when they don't get their way; six-year-olds hurling vile curses at their parents and teachers; ten-year-olds becoming belligerently defiant when their parents tell them to do something. There seems to be no end to the outrageous behavior that is pouring forth from today's children. This simply cannot be explained in terms of inheritance. It can only be explained thus: *Two vastly different child-rearing styles, based on two vastly different child-rearing paradigms, will yield two vastly different child-rearing outcomes.*

As we've already determined, Postmodern Psychological Parenting and traditional biblical child rearing have nothing in common. They are, in fact, antithetical. The former was doomed from the outset. The latter worked well for thousands of years and was showing no signs of senility or breakdown when it was abandoned in the late 1960s and early 1970s. Yes, there were bad parents before the psychological parenting revolution, but bad parents were not a product of a bad paradigm. They were a product of their own badness. The biblical paradigm is perfect, but it does not prevent imperfection on the part of parents. The psychological paradigm is not just imperfect, but was from the start a disaster in the making. And because it is based on falsehoods, it cannot be fixed.

FOOD FOR THOUGHT

Human beings are imperfect; therefore, we cannot do anything with perfection. But imperfect beings following a perfect plan will do a vastly better job than imperfect beings following a plan that is 100 percent defective.

Children have always, from time immemorial, been mischievous. I call that the Adam and Eve Syndrome (AES): A child waits until he thinks adults aren't looking and then does what he's been told not to do. That's human nature; it's not going to change. What's changed is that all too many of today's kids are beyond mischievous—they are hazards to themselves and others.

Fifty and more years ago in the history of Western civilization, the typical four-year-old child was obedient, responsible, and in possession of good self-control. How did parents accomplish that? If Grandma was not using behavior modification to achieve good behavior, what then was she using?

The answer to that question lies in the literal meaning of the word *discipline,* which is "to create a disciple." From that point of view, discipline is the process by which parents transform a willful child into a willing disciple—someone who will look up to them, trust them, subscribe to their values, and follow their lead. This is accomplished not by manipulating consequences, but by providing the child with effective leadership.

Now we're onto something! Discipline is not reward-ship or

punishment-ship or method-ship or consequence-ship—discipline is leadership! We're onto something *big*, in fact, because the principles that define effective leadership and the qualities that make for good leaders do not change from one leadership context to another. What makes for effective leadership in a corporate or church setting also makes for effective leadership in a child-rearing setting. Said another way, if you understand how to lead an adult, then you understand how to lead a child, and you understand, therefore, how to discipline a child. One does not become an effective leader of adults by mastering various behavior modification technologies, nor is that how one becomes an effective leader of children. Leadership is an attitude. It's a mind-set, not a methodology.

It's a Matter of Presentation

Effective leaders—people who have a knack for making other people *want* to follow their lead—are distinguished not by how cleverly they manipulate reward and punishment, but by the following:

- They may disapprove of what you *do,* but they always approve of *you* (unconditional positive regard).

- They lead through example. They do not expect others to do what they have not themselves done or are unwilling to do.

- They are enthusiastic concerning their vision, and their enthusiasm is *communicable.*

- They motivate others to follow their lead through positive coaching and encouragement, by helping people reach down inside themselves and bring out the best in themselves. And because they help people become the very best they can be, those people look up to them.

- They are decisive and willing to make unpopular decisions.

- They "stay the course" when the going gets rough.

In summary, good leaders act as if they know what they are doing, where they are going, and how they are going to get there. Furthermore, good leaders act as if they have every confidence in the world that the people they are charged with leading will, in fact, follow.

I said that to a group of parents once, and one parent exclaimed, "But, John, there are times when I don't know what I'm doing, where I'm going, or how to get there!"

I answered: "The key word is *act*. Good leaders *act* as if they know what they're doing. Of course you don't always know what you're doing, much less its outcome. No good leader does. Leadership sometimes involves making hopeful predictions. But a good leader always, no matter what, *acts* as if he has no doubt concerning the correctness of his decisions."

In other words, proper leadership—including the disciplining of a child—is primarily a matter of *presentation*. Effective leaders are decisive. They project confidence, purpose, and a positive outlook. They *command* the attention of people, and they *command* proper behavior on the part of the people they lead. With regard to the latter, effective leaders always exercise command in a calm, confident manner. People in leadership positions—this includes parents, mind you—who find themselves always having to *demand* attention and proper behavior are doing so because they have not learned how to *command.*

Charisma

I know of a teacher who specifically asks to be assigned the most ill-behaved children in the school, children who have run over other teachers. She has no problems with these kids. If you go into her classroom and observe, as I have done, you'll see that she controls her class through force of personality. She has *charisma,* which the *American Heritage Dictionary* defines as "a personal quality attributed to *leaders* who arouse devotion and enthusiasm" (emphasis mine). This teacher's students are indeed devoted to her, and unlike any teacher before her, she is able to cause them to be enthusiastic about learning. The "worst" kids in the school end up being some of the best students because of her—that word again—*leadership.* She doesn't control her class by manipulating reward and punishment. She controls her class with her determined sense of purpose. When a child in her class misbehaves, for example, she simply stops what she is doing and looks at the child until he regains self-control. Then she asks, "Do you want to say something to the entire class?" at which point the child stands up, turns to look at his or her classmates, and says, "I'm sorry." Now, *that's* charisma! That's leadership! That's what discipline is all about!

You'll find a teacher like her in nearly every school in America—teachers who have few discipline problems with children other teachers have all but given up on. If you observe these teachers in action, you will not be watching people who are using behavior modification techniques. They discipline through their leadership. They have mastered the art of commanding; therefore, they are never demanding. The same is true of parents who have disciplined (discipled) their children properly—they have done so by leading properly, not by using consequences properly.

Think about this for a second. Chances are the parents you know with the best-behaved children are also the calmest, least frazzled parents. Contrary to what some folks may think, these parents are not calm and composed because God arbitrarily blessed or purposefully rewarded them with children who were "easy." Their children are as capable of rebellion as anyone else's. They are calm and composed because whether they even realize it or not, they have mastered the art of "leadership discipline."

The word used in Scripture to denote the importance of parental leadership is "rod." It's going to come as a surprise to many a reader to learn that "the rod" of Bible verses such as Proverbs 13:24—"He who spares the rod hates his son, but he who loves him is careful to discipline him"—is not a spanking. It is leadership. To "spare the rod" is to be lax in one's leadership of one's child. And note also that love and leadership are inseparable. The truly loving parent is one who provides not just ample nurturing, but effective discipline, effective leadership.

But I left some of you hanging, didn't I? I just said one of the most surprising things I could have said—that "the rod" of Scripture is not, by a long shot, a spanking—and then just went right on as if no defense of that position was required. But a defense is indeed required, so allow me.

THE "ROD" OF LEADERSHIP

When non-Christians hear the term "Christian parenting," they are likely to have the following knee-jerk reaction: "Oh, that's about 'sparing the rod and spoiling the child,' isn't it?" Although simplistic, it's an understandable association. After all, some of the best-known Christian parenting experts have placed significant emphasis on the role of spankings in the overall discipline of children, citing such passages as Proverbs 13:24 (above) and Proverbs 22:15 (NASB): "Foolishness is bound in the heart of the child; the rod of discipline will remove it far from him."

Because of this unfortunate emphasis, many Christian parents also believe that God is being very specific on this point: Spankings are his preferred method of punishing children, especially when the misbehavior in question is rebellious or disrespectful. They believe, further, that said spankings should be administered with variations on the rod, which include switches, belts, and paddles.

As a believing and very sincere friend of mine put it, "Quite obviously, God is instructing parents to discipline, and to discipline with spankings."

Is he?

The Bible According to the Bible

According to biblical scholars, one can only ascertain the true meaning of a word, term, or phrase found in the Bible by taking the time to research its use across the whole of Scripture. In biblical exegesis (critical interpretation), consistency reveals meaning. As one biblical scholar has succinctly put it, "Scripture interprets Scripture." When one applies this exegetical formula to the word "rod," two entirely separate categories of meaning become apparent: metaphorical and concrete.

- When the word "rod" is being employed as a metaphor, it is always preceded by the article "the," as in Lamentations 3:1: "I am the man who has seen affliction by the rod of his wrath." In this example, "the rod" is God's righteousness.

- When "rod" is preceded by the article "a," however, it is always with reference to a concrete object—a straight stick that might have been used as a tool of measurement (1 Samuel 17:7; Revelation 21:16), a symbol of authority (Isaiah 14:5), a threshing stick (Isaiah 28:27), or a staff used in herding sheep (Leviticus 27:32). The sole exception to this rule is found in 2 Samuel 7:14, where a tangible rod is referred to as "the rod of men."

Perhaps the most striking example of the difference is found by comparing Exodus 21:20 and Proverbs 23:13. The former, part of the Law, specifies the penalty to be imposed "if a man beats his male or female slave with a rod, and the slave dies as a direct result." Obviously, this rod is not figurative. It is very real. The latter, however, reads, "Do not withhold discipline from a child; if you punish him with the rod, *he will not die*" (emphasis mine).

Reading these two passages, one should be moved to ask, if in fact these two rods are both concrete objects, how can something capable of killing a strong adult slave hold absolutely no potential of being fatal to a child (remember that Proverbs 23:13 is a promise from God himself!). The only way of reconciling the seeming contradiction is to understand that Exodus refers to an object (*a* rod), while Proverbs refers to a quality, an attribute (*the* rod).

In every single instance where the word "rod" is used in connection with the discipline of children, it is preceded by the article "the"; therefore, it is being used figuratively, metaphorically—*not* in reference to something capable of causing physical pain or injury, much less death.

So what is this quality? What is *rod*like discipline? Metaphors borrow their meaning from the concrete. So, for example, the metaphorical use of "slow train" as in "there's a slow train coming" refers to a powerful, virtually unstoppable force with somewhat ominous significance. In other words, understanding the concrete nature of a train that is moving slowing, inexorably, toward some destination is prerequisite to comprehending the metaphor. Likewise, understanding the ancient uses to which rods could be put allows us to understand what is meant by "the rod of discipline."

A Rod by Any Other Name

In Scripture, a rod was (a) a symbol of legitimate authority (for example, a king's scepter), (b) a straight stick or pole used to ensure that measurements were consistent and true, (c) a threshing stick used to separate useful grain from useless chaff, and (d) a staff used to herd domesticated animals into one general area and compel them to move from one place to another. Used metaphorically, therefore, rodlike discipline (a) emanates from a legitimate authority, (b) is consistent and true (it does not waver), (c) separates right behavior from wrong behavior, and (d) establishes boundaries and compels action or change. Taken together, the reference is clearly to leadership.

Further understanding of the metaphor can be had by noting that "the rod" is also used to refer to God's righteousness, as in Lamentations (above) and Isaiah 11:4, where the Lord is described as smiting the earth with "the rod of his mouth." Rodlike child discipline, therefore, is righteous. It is in keeping with the righteous nature of God's discipline of us, his children both adult and child, and consistent with his plan for us.

Don't misunderstand me, please. I am not arguing against spankings per se. I happen to believe that a properly administered spanking can be an appropriate example of the rod. Spankings have their place, but they are not the be-all and end-all of discipline. In fact, nowhere in the whole of Scripture does God prescribe a specific form of discipline for children. He only emphasizes, time and time again, that to be effective, discipline must embody certain characteristics (for example, consistency, per Deuteronomy 6:6–7) and emanate from a legitimate authority figure who is acting with righteousness, in his stead.

Therefore, the mere fact that a parent spanks does not mean his discipline has been "rodlike." A spanking delivered impulsively, in anger, definitely fails to meet the standard. The angry, out-of-control parent is not acting righteously. His impulsive outburst is self-righteous. It communicates his anger, but it is unlikely to do anything but cause resentment on the part of his child. That sort of spanking is an example of what Paul was re-

ferring to when, in his letter to the Ephesians, he exhorted fathers to not "exasperate" their children. Parents exasperate their
children whenever they behave toward them in an exasperated
fashion, which certainly fits with spankings that are delivered
impulsively and out of anger.

*Fathers, do not exasperate your children; instead, bring
them up in the training and instruction of the Lord.*
—*EPHESIANS 6:4*

These understandings will, I hope, serve to free parents from
a narrow approach to discipline such as might result from a literal interpretation of "the rod of discipline" and enable them to
match their specific disciplinary response to the nature of any
specific misbehavior and the context in which it occurs. After
all, is it not inconceivable that God wants parents to spank in
response to every instance of misbehavior? How could God in
his infinite wisdom and mercy demand spankings for misbehavior as disparate as a child's belligerently refusing to clean his
room and a child's simply forgetting to clean his room? Both require discipline, but the same response to both events would reflect neither mercy nor good sense, much less wisdom.

Understanding the difference between *a* rod and *the* rod also
leads to the realization that discipline and punishment are not
one and the same. There will certainly be times when it will be
necessary, right, and just for you to punish your child, but as we

will see, punitive expressions of your leadership should be the exception, not the rule.

TO SPANK OR NOT TO SPANK

The issue of spanking is a controversial one, of course. Unfortunately, any discussion of the pros and cons of spanking is likely to devolve into a shouting match, even (or especially) when the discussion is between professionals. The usual antispanking argument consists of three equally misleading assertions:

1. Spankings are likely to escalate into child abuse.

2. Spankings teach children that it's okay to hit people who upset you.

3. There is always an alternative to spanking.

Not one of these claims is grounded in solid science or even good anecdotal evidence. They don't even make good common sense. That's because they are based on emotion, nothing more. Unfortunately, the media pay lots of attention to spanking research that claims to find dramatic outcomes (that have emotional appeal) and give short shrift to spanking research that finds otherwise. The end result is a growing number of people who believe that spanking is abhorrent.

More Questions Than Answers

There is good reason to believe that most, if not all, of the research that fuels antispanking arguments is tainted by ideological bias on the part of the researchers in question. The best-known spanking research has been done by Murray Straus at the Family Research Institute in New Hampshire. Straus claims that his research proves spanking is associated with high levels of aggression, even criminality. But Straus is also an advocate of laws that would prohibit parents from spanking. When a researcher becomes an advocate for a political cause, it goes without saying that he has checked his objectivity at the door. The research conducted by people without bias—psychologist Robert Larzelere (Straus's former research assistant), for example—has failed to find that spankings per se place children at risk for later social problems.

For example, no compelling evidence exists that might even come close to supporting the notion that spankings cause children to believe hitting is an acceptable way of dealing with frustration or conflict. The most aggressive children, researchers have found, tend to be those who are never spanked! One study, done a number of years ago, found that aggression in children was most closely associated with permissive parenting. That makes common sense, as does most good social science. Children are antisocial by nature. Hitting is antisocial. Permissive parents are less likely than authoritative parents to succeed at persuading their children to restrain antisocial impulses. Voilà! No mystery there.

The Facts Speak

Here are a few more facts:

- Spankings seem to be most effective between ages two and six. Parents who are spanking children older than six, especially if the spankings are frequent, need to take sober stock of their overall approach to discipline.

- Spanking is most effective when paired with another consequence, such as removal of privilege.

- Spankings do not easily or normally escalate into child abuse. Of the many parents who spank, a minuscule number actually wind up abusing their children. In fact, the relationship between spanking and child abuse is paradoxical. Sweden outlawed parental spanking in 1979. A decade or so later, Bob Larzelere conducted a follow-up study in which he found that child abuse had increased significantly since the ban! As mentioned earlier but worth repeating, psychologist Diana Baumrind—considered the foremost researcher in the area of parenting style outcomes—has found that parents who are philosophically opposed to spanking are more likely to overreact to their children's misbehavior than parents who have no such philosophical objection.

- The more often a child is spanked, the less effective any given spanking will be. Children who are spanked frequently often appear to "immunize" to them.

- In 1996, a special conference convened by the American Academy of Pediatrics came to the conclusion that research purporting to prove that spanking incites antisocial behavior was less compelling than research showing that spankings deter antisocial behavior. The committee concluded that there was no evidence to suggest that spankings per se are harmful.

As for the "there's always an alternative to spanking" argument, the begging question becomes, "Is the alternative going to be more effective?" Take the case of a four-year-old who, in a fit of pique, spits at his mother. Which of the following two punishments is more likely to persuade the child to never spit on his mother again: ten minutes in time-out or a spanking? That's a no-brainer, eh? Is it in the child's best interest that he be stopped, as effectively as possible, from ever spitting on his mother again? That's another no-brainer. My point is that the "alternative" argument is likely to be hoist by its own sentimental petard.

Spanking How-tos

Since "the rod" is metaphorical, there is no sound reason to believe that in order to qualify as properly biblical a spanking should be delivered with a paddle, belt, or switch. In fact, I believe the hand is the only appropriate means of administering a spanking, for the simple reason that the spanker's hand feels the pain along with the child, and thus will the spanker know when enough is enough. Needless to say, paddles and the like do not deliver that feedback. Some say that one's hand should only be associated with affection and that spanking with the hand will cause the child confusion. I respect their concerns, and I certainly agree that confusion is likely if spankings occur explosively, but I don't believe there's good reason to think that a child who is properly spanked (see below) will be confused when the same parent who spanked him with his hand embraces him with loving arms when the spanking is over. That's certainly confirmed by my experience. When I spanked, I used my hand. My children did not draw away from me in fear when I reached out my hand to show them affection.

Spankings should not be delivered in anger, but they should be delivered righteously. A child who is about to be spanked should know that the parent is seriously displeased. In that regard, spanking should be reserved for the most serious of offenses, including belligerent demonstrations of disrespect toward or defiance of parents or other legitimate authority figures, stealing, lying that was hurtful to others (bearing false witness), and assault.

In most cases, the parent should sit down with the child and make sure the child knows why what he or she did was wrong and why the parent has decided on a spanking—to wit, to emphasize the seriousness of the offense. With toddlers, however, there are certainly times when a swift pop or two to the rear, without a prior conversation or even so much as a warning, will be appropriate. In those cases, spanking is designed not so much to correct the behavior that's taking place, but to quickly terminate a misbehavior and get the child's attention. Ideally, spankings should take place in a private place, such as the child's room, and the parent should stay with the child until his or her distress has passed, at which time the parent should reassure the child of the parent's abiding love.

Unfortunately, most parents do not spank according to the above guidelines, which is why most spankings, while they do not qualify as harmful, much less abusive, nonetheless qualify as meaningless. They are delivered in anger, without patient explanation, without reassurance, and entirely too often. For all those reasons they accomplish absolutely nothing, as attested to by the significant number of parents who report that they spank over and over and over again for the same misbehavior.

Again, it is not my intention to advocate for or against spankings. They are not essential to proper discipline, nor are they illegitimate per se. I can't say it enough: Effective discipline is not conveyed by methods, spanking or otherwise, but through effective communication of instructions and expectations—through leadership.

CODA

The week I was finishing this book, the California state legislature began debating a proposed law that would prohibit parental spanking of children under age four. The law would make spanking a child under the age of three a crime punishable by a fine and/or jail time.

"I think it's pretty hard to argue you need to beat a child three years old or younger," said Sally Lieber, the Democratic assemblywoman (San Francisco) who is the main mover and shaker behind the bill.

I agree with that. In fact, I'll expand that to include any age child. But of course Lieber is using "beat" to mean any swat to a child's rear parts, and in so doing she is revealing a predilection for emotional hyperactivity, the province of the demagogue. Every state in the Union prohibits the beating of children. To equate spanking per se with child abuse is demagoguery.

Lieber probably believes herself to be a champion for children. In fact, she may be doing children a grave disservice, to which the studies cited above attest. The proposed law targeted only parents who spank kids three and under, and Lieber wisely withdrew it before it reached debate. Nevertheless, this is a harbinger of things to come. For antispanking hysterics, Lieber's law was only a test case. The real intent is to insert government into the parent-child relationship and eliminate parental discretion in discipline. People like Lieber will keep trying. If they eventually succeed, antispanking law will put us on a slippery slope leading straight to Hillary Clinton's collectivist "village," where the elite few—as wryly expressed by columnist Thomas Sowell—"impose their superior wisdom and virtue on parents."[2]

A warning from Supreme Court Justice Louis Brandeis (1856–1941) seems particularly appropriate: "The greatest dangers to liberty lurk in insidious encroachment by men of zeal, well-meaning but without understanding."

Questions for Group Discussion or Personal Reflection

1. Have you been a believer in behavior modification? If so, can you identify the problems that belief has caused in your attempts to properly discipline your children?

2. Does your parenting style match the description of effective leadership given in this chapter? What do you need to change about your parenting style to become a more effective leader of children?

3. Are you a "charismatic" parent? If not, do you know a charismatic parent? If so, write down five qualities that person projects that define his or her charisma. Here's one to get you started: *She doesn't get the least bit ruffled when one of her children becomes upset over a decision she has made, no matter how upset the child becomes.* In what specific ways does her parenting style differ from yours?

4. Did you think that the biblical "rod" meant a spanking? How does it change your parenting point of view to see it as a metaphor for leadership? How will that change in point of view change your parenting behavior?

5. If you have overly relied on spankings, how will you now handle some of the misbehavior for which you have spanked?

CHAPTER ELEVEN

Command, Compel, Confirm

Come, my children, listen to me; I will teach you the
fear of the LORD.
—PSALM 34:11

A child who gets his own way brings shame to his
mother.
—PROVERBS 29:15 NASB

Those who spare the rod of discipline hate their
children. Those who love their children care enough
to discipline them.
—PROVERBS 13:24 NLT

Authors are fond of coming up with cutesy mnemonic devices to help their audiences remember key concepts, and I
am no different, albeit I maintain that any such devices employed by yours truly are not cutesy, but gripping and dynamic
and the like.

With that in mind, the reader is encouraged to repeat the
following set of three words—each of which begins with the

letter C—three times with dynamic vigor: communication, consequences, consistency. (Remember to say them two more times to fully implant the mnemonic effect.)

Those C-words are the building blocks of effective discipline. By themselves however, blocks are nothing but lifeless lumps. So, each of these lifeless lumps needs something with which to bring it to life—a modifier! It just so happens that the life-giving modifiers in question also begin with the letter C: command, compel, confirm.

Put 'em all together and what results are the three mnemonically gripping principles of effective discipline:

1. Disciplinary **communication** (communicating instructions, limits, and expectations) must **command**!

2. Disciplinary **consequences** must **compel**.

3. Disciplinary **consistency** must **confirm** the parent's determination to further the best interests of the child in question.

At this point, you are no doubt feeling gripped and invigorated and ready to get out there and do some great discipline with your child!

In this chapter, you'll learn that each of these three all-important principles is confirmed in the Bible, the only parenting book Grandma ever needed. You'll also learn how to translate each principle into effective behavior so that you can begin "Parenting by The Book" and reaping the rewards God promises to those who live according to his instruction.

PRINCIPLE ONE: COMMANDING COMMUNICATION

"All you need say is 'Yes' if you mean yes, 'No' if you mean no; anything more than this comes from the Evil One" (Matthew 5:37 NJB).

In the Sermon on the Mount, Jesus gave his disciples what is without question the most important of all leadership principles: Say what you mean, mean what you say, and do what you say you are going to do. (This, by the way, happens to be an excellent definition of "integrity.")

Do your children know that your word can be relied upon, that it is the law? Does each of them know, beyond a shadow of doubt, that when you say yes you mean nothing short of yes? Do they know that when you say no you mean no? More precisely:

- When you tell one of your children that you expect him to do something, does he absolutely *know* that he is going to have to do it, that you absolutely *will* enforce your instructions? If you can answer that question with an unqualified yes, then your child has learned that your yes indeed means yes. On the other hand, have you given your child reason to think that if he stalls long enough, complains loudly and dramatically enough, or begins to argue you may give up and do it yourself? If that's the case, then your child has learned that your yes really means "I wish you would."

- When you tell one of your children that you will *not* let him do something he wants to do or give him something he desires, does he absolutely, without a doubt know that you mean what you have said? If that's the case, then he has learned that your no means no. Or does he have reason to believe that if he argues, cries pitifully, or begins ranting, raving, and raging, you are very likely to give in, if not completely, at least partially? If that's the case, then you have taught your child that your no doesn't mean no; it means "I'd rather you didn't," "I'd rather not," or "Please don't make this difficult, okay?"

"Some Say I'm a Dreamer"

Relevant to this discussion is the phenomenon of the so-called argumentative child. Although a good number of parents have told me they live with such children, there really is no such thing. There are only children who have learned that (a) their parents will argue with them, and (b) the outcomes of said arguments are likely to be in their favor. In other words, these children simply take advantage of opportunities their argumentative parents present to them.

The parents in question all make the same mistake: When their children demand explanations, they give explanations. When their children do not like decisions they've made, they try to persuade their children to agree with them. That attempt has never and is never going to come to anything because of one simple fact: *If a child does not like a decision a parent has made, the child is not going to like the reason the parent gives for the decision, and nothing the parent says is going to change that.*

Argumentative parents cannot seem to accept that reality. They think they can explain themselves cleverly enough to change a child who doesn't like a parental decision into a child who likes it. For some odd reason, these parents think they can succeed where no parent before them has ever succeeded. They think it's possible to bring about the following sort of exchange between a parent and a child:

Child: "Mom, can I go to the quarry with my friends?"

Mom: "No, you can't."

Child: "Why not!?"

Mom: "A child drowned there last week."

Child: "But Mom, I know how to swim!"

Mom: "So did the child who drowned. Studies on drowning find that most people who drown know how to swim. The problem is that they get too tired, or have a cramp, or when they dive in the water they hit something that knocks the air out of them. Furthermore, most people drown in bodies of water where there is no lifeguard, and there is no lifeguard at the quarry. For all those reasons, you can't go. Period."

Child: "Mom, I truly appreciate that explanation. I was mad a minute ago, but you've convinced me that going to the quarry with my friends is a really bad idea. I'm lucky to have you for a mom. Thanks."

That sort of dialogue between parent and child is an impossible dream. Argumentative parents, therefore, are dreamers. They have their heads in the clouds of idealism. A child, by definition, cannot understand and appreciate an adult point of view, and no amount of words, however eloquent, will change that. Parents who think they can succeed where no parent has succeeded before have only themselves to blame when they fail.

Likewise, there is no such thing as a child who cannot take no for an answer. There are only children who have learned that when their parents say no, all they have to do is throw conniption fits and no will probably change to "Oh, all right!" These are parents who cannot say no and mean it. They blame their children for their own shortcomings because passing the buck is a human tradition that's as old as the proverbial hills.

> *"Who told you that you were naked?" he asked. "Have you been eating from the tree I forbade you to eat?"*
> *The man replied, "It was the woman you put with me; she gave me some fruit from the tree, and I ate it."*
> —GENESIS 3:11–12 (NJB)

Just the Ticket

If a certain poll I take with my audiences is any indication, it would appear that most parents have taught their children that arguments and fits are tickets to getting their way.

In 2006, I was speaking in Des Moines, Iowa, before a church audience of some five hundred people, when I decided to find out if my intuitions along these lines were true. After reading what Jesus said in Matthew 5:37, I asked for a show of hands from those parents who could say with absolute certainty that when they say yes their children know they mean yes, and when they say no their children know they mean no. About ten hands, representing 2 percent of the audience, went up, some of them tentatively. I then asked, "Now raise your hand if *your parents* would have raised *their* hands to that question." At least three hundred hands went up.

"That's precisely why," I then said, "your parents had far fewer hassles with discipline than you are having. It's not because you were easier than are your children; it's because your parents exercised more effective leadership over you than you are exercising over your children. Some three hundred of you learned that your parents' word was law. Except for ten of you, your kids have not learned the same thing about your word."

I've since repeated that exercise with dozens of audiences, large and small. The results—relative to audience size—have never varied much from that first time in Des Moines. Would you raise your hand to the first question? Would you raise your hand on your parents' behalf?

When "No" Means "Maybe"

Children have not changed over the past thirty years, but child rearing certainly has. The discipline problems so many of today's parents are having with their children are not the result of brain chemicals that are out of whack or brain malfunctions that cause children to hear the word "maybe" when their parents have actually said no. The problem is parents themselves, parents who have fallen for the promises of Postmodern Psychological Parenting. If you are one of the parents in question, and there's a good likelihood you are, then this is actually good news, because it means that you can finally begin solving the discipline problems you are having with your child.

You've been beating your head against the wall, trying to change your can't-take-no-for-an-answer, argumentative child into a child who accepts no for an answer and doesn't try to engage you in arguments, haven't you? And all you've gotten for your efforts is a bruised forehead and a monstrous headache, right? That's because the problem is not your child; the problem is *you*. You've been trying to change the wrong person! Can you accept that? If your answer is yes and this yes truly means yes, then it won't be long before your headache and your bruises will begin to disappear! The cure is really quite simple; so simple that you're going to wonder why you didn't think of it yourself.

It consists of three steps:

1. When your child asks for something, and you say he can't have it or do it, and your child demands an explanation, as in, "Why not?!" give one of the only six reasons there are: (1) You're not old enough, (2) you might get hurt, (3) we don't have the money (or will not use it that way), (4) we don't have the time (or won't take the time) for that, (5) we don't believe in that (our values don't allow that), (6) we don't like those kids.

2. When you have given your chosen reason in five words or less, and your child stomps his foot and yells out that he doesn't agree with your reason, thinks it's dumb, or wants to tell you why you should change your mind, simply look at him with great compassion and say, "If I was your age, I wouldn't like that decision either."

3. Then turn around and walk away, leaving your child to—I'm going to steal one of Grandma's favorite lines—"stew in his own juices."

See how easy that is? Those three simple steps will stop arguments over no before they begin. Notice that there is a difference between giving a reason (right and proper) and trying to reason (trying to convince the child that your reason is valid, which is fruitless). Let's revisit the prior example:

Child: "Mom, can I go to the quarry with my friends?"

Mom: "No, you can't."

Child: "Why not?!"

Mom: "Because the quarry is a dangerous place for children to be without adult supervision." (A combination of answers 1 and 2 above.)

Child: "No, it's not! No one has ever gotten hurt going there! Besides, I'll be careful, Mom, I promise."

Mom: "You know, if I was you, and my mother told me I couldn't go to the quarry with my friends, I'd be upset, too, and I'd promise her the same thing. And she would still say no, and I'm still saying no, and nothing you say will get me to change my mind, but you're welcome to find that out for yourself." (At which point, Mom turns away and goes back to what she was doing. If her child persists, then every so often Mom will turn around, fix her child with a steely gaze, say no in the calmest of voices, and turn away.)

That's how a child learns that no means no. Don't expect a one-day miracle, however. This learning may take weeks, depending on the thickness of the child's skull and the amount of wax that's accumulated in his ears. But this simple cure will eventually penetrate even the thickest skull and earwax that has turned to concrete.

Now we come to arguments over yes: e.g., when you tell your child to do something and he demands to know why he, the unrecognized emperor of the universe, has to stoop so low. Grandma stopped these arguments before they started with four deadly words: "Because I said so."

"Because I Said So"

Mom: "Charlie, I need you to take out the garbage, please."

Charlie: "Why do I have to take out the smelly garbage?"

Mom: "Because I said so." (At which point, Mom resumes doing what she was doing. It is vital, you see, that this be done with complete nonchalance.)

The purveyors of Postmodern Psychological Parenting told parents that "Because I said so" was a bad thing to say. It stomped on a child's curiosity and "right to know" (where this right originated is still a mystery), thwarted his intellectual development, made him feel that his point of view didn't count, and thus lowered his self-esteem. None of that is true, of course. Children of my generation heard those four words a fair amount. We were still supremely curious. We did better in school than today's kids, so it must not have interfered with our ability to think. We suffered much less depression than do today's kids, so it must not have caused any harm to our psyches. Nevertheless, parents believed the new experts, and as a consequence, arguments between parents and children are the stuff of today's families.

These are the facts: "Because I said so" is a statement of leadership. It affirms a parent's authority. It says "the discussion is over."

For those reasons, it prevents argument between parent and child, and that is always a good thing—for parent *and* child.

Do effective leaders do much explaining when it comes to their decisions? No, they do not. To put a decision into proper context, a leader might give a brief reason (noun), but he does not try to reason (verb). He does not explain the thought process by which he arrived at the decision because the minute he does so, two things happen: First, he begins to look as if he's really not sure of himself, and second, he invites people to begin questioning whether his decision is the best decision possible. Another way of saying the same thing: Leadership demands decisiveness, and when people in leadership positions begin giving explanations, they look less than decisive. It is, in fact, more important for a leader to be always decisive than for him to be always right. Besides, it is possible to be always decisive; it is impossible for anyone to always be right.

Politicians explain themselves because they're trying to persuade people to agree with them. Politicians want people's approval. Leaders just state themselves. They are not trying to persuade; rather, they are exercising command, and leaders are not looking for approval. Politicians are afraid to make unpopular decisions. Leaders are not. In the face of uproar over an unpopular decision, a politician is likely to reverse course. In the face of uproar over an unpopular decision, a leader stays the course. It goes without saying that many parents are more like politicians than they are leaders. What about you? Are you a politician-parent or a leader-parent?

Jesus told his disciples (and us) to make sure that when they said yes they truly meant yes and when they said no they truly meant no because he was training them to become leaders, to take up his cross and make disciples of others. He was telling them that when they spoke to others about him, when they shared the Good News of his coming, they must be sure to speak with complete confidence that what they were saying was the Truth, the whole Truth, and nothing but the Truth. In order to create no doubt, he knew they must speak with clarity and without equivocation. Jesus's advice applies to anyone who is in position of leadership, and that includes parents.

It's All in the Telling

A mother once told me that her five-year-old daughter wouldn't do anything she, the mother, told her to do. I was incredulous.

"I've never known a five-year-old who wouldn't do what she was told," I said. "Most of the time, that is, but most of the time is all you're ever going to get with human beings, especially children."

"Well, you've never met my daughter," she rejoined, "because my daughter won't do *anything* I tell her to do. I've tried *everything*, and she still won't do what I tell her to do!"

"I'll bet you don't *tell* her to do anything," I said.

"What do you mean?"

"I mean, if you're like most of today's parents, you plead, bargain, bribe, cajole, reason, explain, and threaten. You don't just *tell*. When you stop pleading and the like, and you begin *telling*, your daughter will begin doing what you tell her to do."

She thought a few seconds, then said, "Have you been hiding in our house?"

This mother did not realize that the problem she was having with her daughter was a problem *she* had created. She had tried every conceivable reward, punishment, method, technique, and strategy, and her daughter had only grown more stubborn. In her conversation with me (there was more), she began to realize that in trying to change her daughter she was barking up the wrong tree. Yes, her daughter was stubborn, but before her hardheadedness could be dealt with properly, Mom had to first learn how to properly convey instructions; how to *tell*.

A couple of years ago, our daughter, Amy, and her husband left their youngest child, Holden, with us for five days. At the time, Holden was in the midst of his most terrible, horrible twos—according to his parents at least. Amy described Holden as a "screamer" who had to have everything his way. Willie and I listened politely, as good grandparents should in such circumstances, but we knew why Holden screamed. His parents *cared* if he screamed. Holden was going to discover that Willie and I did not care. And sure enough, not once during his five-day visit did Holden the Horrible ever scream. He never cried. He never so much as whimpered. He never even *looked* as if he was about to whimper. The whole time he was with us, he accepted the way things were, did what we told him to do, and adapted to our lifestyle quite nicely. When we told Amy the good news, she said Holden wasn't accustomed to us. He was still trying to figure us out. The truth is Holden figured us out in a matter of hours. He figured out that when we said yes we meant yes, and when we said no we meant no. He figured out that screaming wasn't going to work with us, that we didn't care if he screamed. And he was a much more content little boy for having figured that out.

Willie and I didn't reward Holden for not screaming. We didn't make any effort to keep him happy. We just *told* him what we were doing and what he was going to do. For five days, we were Leaders of Holden the Former Horrible, and leadership, as I've said but can't say enough, is all in the telling.

Leadership Is Not for Milquetoasts

The root word of discipline is "disciple." In the strictest sense of the term, then, discipline is the process by which parents transform a self-centered little rebel who wants to believe the universe revolves around him into a willing *disciple* who willingly puts his parents at the center of his universe. In fact, instead of saying that parents should properly discipline their children, it is more accurate to say that parents should properly *disciple* them. That discipling is accomplished through leadership, and leadership in any context is largely a matter of how effectively one communicates instructions, rules, expectations, and boundaries. Good leaders, wherever they are found, are masters of "leadership speech," speech that is:

- Clear—direct, unambiguous, plain, free of abstractions.

- Concise—economical.

- Commanding—authoritative, assertive.

Using the example of a mother who wants her four-year-old child to stick close to her in a crowded store, the following is an example of leadership speech: "While we are in this store, you will stay right next to me at all times. Do you understand?"

This, by contrast, is *not* leadership speech: "Please don't make me run after you in this store, okay? It's dangerous, for one thing. You could get lost and some strange man could grab you away and do things to you. So please don't run away from me, okay? If you stay with me, Mommy will buy you an ice cream cone on the way home, okay?"

It should be obvious that the nineteen words in the first example are vastly more effective than the fifty-nine words used in the second. The former is clear, concise, and commanding; the latter is vague, verbose, and void of command.

Unfortunately, many if not most parents, when giving their children instructions, are likely to sound like the mom in the second example—they use what I call "Milquetoast speech," named after Caspar Milquetoast,[1] a comic strip character who never seemed able to speak his mind clearly, much less assertively. Let's listen in on a Milquetoast Mom who wants her four-year-old to pick up his toys:

"I have some company coming over, sweetheart, and it would really help Mommy if you would stop playing and pick up these toys, okay? If you'll do that for Mommy, you can have a bowl of ice cream afterward. Would you like some ice cream? Okay then, you have to pick up these toys. Ice cream is for good boys who pick up their toys. Do you think you need some help? Yes? Oh, I don't think so. You carried the toys here, so you should be able to pick them up, don't you think? Honey? I'm asking you something? Are you paying attention to me? Sweetheart? Please pick up these toys now, okay, so Mommy doesn't have to do it, okay? I'm asking you nicely, aren't I? Honey? Sweetheart, my company will be here any minute now, and these toys really need to be off the floor by the time they get here. Let's pick them up together, okay? Sweetie, Mommy needs your help picking up these toys. I shouldn't have to pick them up by myself. Okay?"

If that sounded familiar, the good news is you are reading the right book. Like that well-meaning mom, parents employ Milquetoast speech whenever they whine, complain, plead, entreat, entice, bribe, and explain themselves persuasively. When none of that works, as will be the case 95 percent of the time, a third form of expression, named after one of the most terrifying movie monsters of all time, is likely to occur. The parent stiffens, begins to tremble, her face morphs into the face of death and destruction, and out comes the Godzilla Screech:

"WHY CAN'T YOU LISTEN AND DO THIS ONE LITTLE THING, JUST THIS ONE TIME, FOR ME!? WHY DO YOU GIVE ME SUCH TROUBLE ABOUT EVERYTHING I ASK!? I'VE HAD IT WITH YOU! IF YOU DON'T START PICKING UP THESE TOYS, RIGHT NOW, I'M GOING TO...TO...I'M GOING TO...THROW THEM ALL AWAY AND WRITE A LETTER TO SANTA TELLING HIM WHAT A BAD BOY YOU ARE AND THAT HE SHOULDN'T BRING YOU ANY MORE TOYS AT CHRISTMAS! AND WHILE I'M AT IT, I'M GOING TO WRITE LETTERS TO THE EASTER BUNNY AND THE TOOTH FAIRY, TOO!"

The predictable juxtaposition of Milquetoast speech and the Godzilla screech sets up a vicious cycle. When Mommy calms down, she feels awful. She worries that her outburst has caused her child debilitating psychological anguish, that it has permanently lowered his self-esteem. (As "proof" of this, at her eruption he ran, weeping, and took refuge in his room.) To atone for her parenting sin, Mommy picks up the toys herself, apologizes to her child ("Mommy's sorry, sweetheart. I'm just having a bad day. Please forgive me."), and promises to take him to the mall for a banana split and an early Christmas present (in May) after her company leaves. And the next time she wants him to do something, she again beats around the bush, and again he pays her no mind, and again she becomes possessed by Godzilla, and again she feels guilty, and again she atones, and around and around they go.

Leadership speech prevents this vicious cycle. Staying with the above example, a Magnificently Motivating Mom (or a Decisively Declarative Dad) would say, "I need you to pick up these toys, right now. I'll be back in a few minutes to see that it's done." (At that point, and without hesitation, MMM [or DDD] turns around and walks away, thus giving her [his] child no "target" at which to aim any resistance.)

Because the instruction is clear, concise, and commanding, the child of a MMM (or DDD) is far more likely than the child of a Milquetoast Mom (or MD) to pick up his toys. But life's not perfect, is it? So a parent asks, "But what if I tell my child, using leadership speech, to do something and he doesn't? He ignores me or just downright defies me! What should I do then?"

The specific answer to that question depends on a number of factors, including the child's age, where the misbehavior takes place, and the history of the problem, but the general answer is that if leadership speech—Plan A—doesn't get the job done, then it's time for Plan B, a consequence.

But before I go any further, please take note of the fact that whereas most parents think consequences are Plan A, they are actually Plan B; they are the backup. Parents who rely exclusively on consequences are forever dealing with some problem or other. They spin their wheels. It goes without saying that they often complain of being stressed out by their children and the disproportionate outpouring of energy it takes to raise them. On the other hand, parents who use consequences only as a backup to leadership speech make lots of progress and usually testify to feeling little parenting stress at all.

When you have to go to Plan B, however, go there with determination, intolerance, and righteousness. The consequences you mete out to your child should always be powerful enough to *compel* him or her to reestablish self-control in a present situation and act correctly in similar future situations. They should cause permanent memories to form. In that regard, they absolutely must be decidedly unpleasant. As you will soon see, the sort of consequences I'm referring to are not the sort generally recommended by the pundits of Postmodern Psychological Parenting, but by now that should come as no surprise.

PRINCIPLE TWO: COMPELLING CONSEQUENCES

"No discipline seems pleasant at the time, but painful. Later on, however, it produces a harvest of righteousness and peace for those who have been trained by it" (Hebrews 12:11).

I am often moved to share the guidance offered by the writer of Hebrews with parents, such as the mother who once asked me how to get their ten-year-old son to stop throwing his belongings all over the living area of their house. When he came home from school, he would toss his jacket on the floor just inside the door, drop his books on the sofa, and kick off his shoes just before he dashed upstairs to change his clothes, which were then strewn everywhere. His mother had pleaded and begged and threatened and rewarded, and nothing—absolutely nothing—had worked. She was at her wit's end. What did I recommend?

I told her that if she was willing to follow my advice to the letter that the problem would be solved within three days at the outside. She said she was ready to do anything.

"The next time he comes home and throws his things all over the downstairs of the house, pick them up," I told her.

"But, John," she exclaimed, "that's exactly what I've been doing!"

"I know," I said, "but you haven't done what I'm about to tell you to do."

"Which is?" she asked expectantly.

"Which is," I said, "after you pick up all of his things and put them where they belong, find your son and show him what you've done. Show him where you put his jacket, his shoes, and his book bag. Then take him to his room and say, 'This is your room, which I've also made nice and tidy because this is where you are staying for the rest of the day, which will be a shorter day than usual because you are going to bed immediately after supper. Also know that in the future, I am never going to nag you about throwing your things around the house. If you don't put something where it belongs, I will, without complaint, and my reward for picking up your things will be a child-free evening.'"

She looked at me incredulously for a few moments and then said, "He has to stay in his room all day and go to bed early just for not putting his things where they belong?"

"When he throws things all over the house," I asked, "who gets upset?"

"Me," she answered.

"Right," I said. *"You* get upset. And as long as *you* are the person who gets upset over this, your son has no reason to ever stop throwing his things all over the house. When *he* is the person who becomes upset because he throws his stuff around, he will start putting his things away properly. I'm simply telling you how to upset him."

In this case, the emotional consequences of the child's lack of responsibility concerning his belongings were being borne by his mother. In other words, the "monkey" of the problem was on her back. To solve the problem, she had to get the monkey off her back and put it where it belonged—on her son's back. After all, no one can tame an unruly monkey except its rightful owner, and no one wants to carry around an unruly monkey.

This mother was taken aback at my recommendation because it didn't sound modern. She never expected such outrageousness to come from a psychologist. She would not have been shocked if I had recommended that she reward him on days he didn't toss his things around and ignore it when he did. She would not have been the least bit surprised if I had told her to fine him a dime for each thing he left lying around. But those approaches would not have resulted in one smidgen of progress. Three weeks into being rewarded, ignored, or fined, her son would have still been scattering his belongings around the house. My recommendation was old-fashioned. It was, in fact, an example of what Grandma called "lowering the boom."[2] The "boom" referred to a consequence that would knock the proverbial wind out of a child; a completely unexpected punishment that would get his attention and create a permanent memory. Theoretically, and usually in fact, the child would never, ever want to experience that particular punishment again. Voilà! The problem was solved.

As I was writing this chapter, the mother of a fifteen-year-old girl asked me (through the members' area of my website at www.rosemond.com) if grounding her daughter for two weeks for stealing seventy-five dollars from her was too much. No, I replied, it was not too much. It was too little. I recommended grounding the daughter for three months, and renewing the term of the grounding at one incident of disobedience or disrespect (meaning she might not be a free spirit again until she went off to college). The girl had used part of the money to have her navel pierced. I advised this mother to tell her daughter that she was free to have a body piercing, but as long as she chose to keep it, she would not get a driver's license. This young lady needed to be taught a lesson she would never forget. I can only hope, for her sake, that her mother found the strength to be the Meanest Mom Ever, Her Most Righteous Momness. In the long run, it's the unforgettable consequences that count.

Unforgettable

Compelling consequences create permanent, decidedly unpleasant memories. A consequence that isn't memorable isn't going to "last." As soon as it's forgotten, the misbehavior will re-emerge from its temporary hiding place, refreshed and ready to do battle.

Nearly everyone in my generation remembers one of his or her parents saying, "I guess it's time for me to do something you'll never forget." Needless to say, the subject at hand was some flagrant misbehavior, and the *something* was sometimes a very painful spanking, but not always. It might have been assignment to some monumental chore—painting the entire outside of the house—during the performance of which the child could not leave the grounds. A friend of mine served this penance at age fifteen. The offense: smoking a cigarette. It was the first and last cigarette my friend ever smoked. My stepfather once required me to write "I will never again come home after dark on a school night" one thousand times! When I was finished, he told me that the next time it happened, I would write the same sentence five thousand times. I believed him, largely because he was being so matter of fact. He might have been saying, "It's raining outside." I never came home after dark on a school night again (until my school-night curfew was so extended). Memories are made of painting the entire house because you got into trouble in school and writing the same sentence one thousand times because you came home after dark—lasting, *painful* memories.

In his letter to the Hebrew Christians the writer used the term "discipline" to mean punishment. He might as well be saying that a consequence that doesn't create a lasting unpleasant memory isn't really punitive. It may be annoying to the child in question, but it's not punitive, and if that's the case, the misbehavior is likely to keep happening. Consequences that fail to create lasting memories produce no lasting persuasive effect.

I am reminded of the parents who, when their five-year-old son rode his new bicycle out of the neighborhood, ending up a mile distant from their home, responded by taking his bike away from him for the rest of that day. Several days later, he again ate of the fruit of knowledge of the world outside his neighborhood. It was not until his parents took his new bicycle away for two months that he stopped wanting to taste that particular fruit. If they'd done that in the first place, they would have saved themselves lots of emotional wear and tear. Furthermore, the "pain" of their message would have saved their son the trouble of having to test their rule over and over again until he discovered they were indeed serious.

Said differently, the punishments parents dole out should *not* "fit" the crimes for which they are doled. They should not be "fair" by contemporary standards. A misbehavior that merits a rank of 3 on a scale of 1 to 10 deserves a punishment that's at least a 6. That greatly increases the likelihood that the misbehavior will enjoy the shortest possible lifespan, which is in everyone's best interest, especially the child's. So if a three-year-old misbehaves at ten o'clock in the morning, I'd have no problem confining him to his room for the remainder of the day.

"But what if he just did something fairly small, John," someone might ask, "like taking a cookie without permission?"

Then he'll think at least twice before taking a cookie without permission again. The problem with thinking that the consequence has to be "fair," that it has to "match" the misbehavior, is that any misbehavior, however small, if not nipped in the proverbial bud, can rapidly grow into something fairly pernicious. A slippery slope sits right in front of every bad behavior. Within a few weeks, taking a cookie without permission can easily escalate into full-blown rebellion against any and all rules. Being confined to his room for eight hours will demonstrate to this three-year-old—at a most opportune time, I might add—that when his parents say no, they mean no. They do not mean, "We wish you wouldn't." In the final analysis, this isn't about taking a cookie; rather, this is about this hypothetical little boy's future. Is he going to be a happy child who obeys the rules or a rebellious malcontent? Remember, disobedient children are not happy children; they are prisoners of their own rebellious natures. For the human spirit, which is creative and cooperative, to rule human nature, rebelliousness must be made to surrender to legitimate authority.

Relevant to this discussion is the fact that time-out is currently the most commonly used consequence and has been for more than thirty years. Mental health professionals promoted time-out as the be-all, end-all consequence. There was a time when even I recommended it liberally. Then I woke up to the fact that time-out works with children who are already well behaved. I woke up to the fact that no parent to whom I recommended time-out had ever reported lasting good results. I've asked numerous audiences of up to one thousand parents, "Raise your hand if time-out cured a major behavioral problem you were having with your child." A hand has yet to appear. People in their seventies and older—Grandma's peers—tell me they think time-out is silly and pointless, and that the person who thought it up must have been from la-la land. Again, mental health professionals strike out and Grandma hits a home run.

Time-out is silly and pointless because it creates no lasting, discomforting memory. It is, in fact, the weakest consequence ever devised. It's fine to use time-out with toddlers, but by the time a child is three, time-out should be replaced by far more powerful, persuasive penalties. Using time-out to deal with a major, long-standing behavioral problem is akin to using a fly swatter to fend off a charging elephant.

Using powerful, persuasive punishments that don't "fit" their crimes greatly diminishes the likelihood that parents will ever lose their cool. In Proverbs 13:24 (NLT), we read, "Those who spare the rod of discipline hate their children. Those who love their children care enough to discipline them." This does not mean that parents show love for children by spanking them. For the purpose of our discussion, it means that when a parent "holds back the rod of discipline" (in whatever form) and tries instead to reason, bribe, threaten, reward, cajole, or time-out a child into behaving properly, the parent's frustration level is sure to go up and up and up until, at some point, the parent "cracks" and unloads on the child in a "hateful," exasperated rage. In this regard, as I mentioned earlier, the best study ever done on discipline styles[3] found that parents who are philosophically opposed to spanking are actually *more likely* to fly into verbal and physical rages toward their children than parents who spank occasionally. For parents to nip misbehavior in the proverbial bud is a kindness to a child, a blessing of untold value.

Do What You Can, When You Can

I was talking with a mother who told me her six-year-old seemed to "time" his misbehavior to occur when she could not punish him.

"For example," she said, "he'll wait until I have to leave the house to run an errand and he'll do something he's not supposed to do, knowing I can't do anything about it."

"Why do you think you can't you do anything about it?" I asked.

"Well," she said, "you have to punish right away for it to mean anything, right? I mean, you can't punish two hours after the fact, right?"

"No, and no," I replied, and went on to point out to her what behavior modification theory—the dominant disciplinary paradigm—obscures: Children aren't dogs. You can't punish a dog two hours after it has misbehaved, but you can certainly punish a six-year-old child two hours after he has misbehaved. You can punish a six-year-old child two days after he's misbehaved! Or even three or four!

It never fails to surprise parents when I tell them that they don't have to punish misbehavior immediately—toddlers being the exception. By the time a child is three years old, memory is beginning to form. From that point on, parents can delay the delivery of consequences for a period of time that is equivalent to the reliable extent of the child's memory. So if a three-year-old misbehaves at ten o'clock in the morning, it's perfectly all right to tell him at six o'clock that he has to go to bed right after supper. In every instance of this sort, the parent needs to describe the precipitating misbehavior clearly, but the memory span of a three-year-old child is at least eight hours long.

By the time a child is five or six years old, consequences can be delayed several days. Again, every time a parent delays a consequence, the parent must describe the misbehavior in question. He or she must "replay" the misbehavior verbally to activate the child's memory, as in, "I'm sending you to bed early today because this morning, when I told you to pick up your toys, you told me that you were not going to. So, I picked them up for you. I hope I don't have to do this ever again, but I will." By age ten, consequences can be delayed a week, and with teens, they can be delayed months. I'm dead serious. The parents of a fifteen-year-old told me that they did not let their child go to summer camp because of an incident that had happened in March of that same year, and they did not inform the child of their decision until a week before camp started. That much of a delay between misbehavior and a consequence isn't something I often recommend, but in this case, the punishment was most definitely appropriate. In most cases, however, even with a teenager, a parent is going to be able to deliver an appropriate consequence within a week or two.

Recap

Before we discuss the importance of consistency, let's review what I've taught you so far in this chapter. It actually amounts to just two things: *tell* and *compel.* To help yourself remember these very complicated and arcane disciplinary principles, I urge you to make a sign that reads *"Tell,* then *compel!"* and put it on your refrigerator. When one of your kids asks you to explain it, just say, "Oh, that's just a reminder of how simple life can be."

PRINCIPLE THREE: CONFIRMING CONSISTENCY

"Fathers, do not exasperate your children; instead, bring them up in the training and instruction of the Lord" (Ephesians 6:4).

In his letter to the Ephesians, my all-time-favorite parenting expert, Paul, said exactly what I've been saying over and over again in this book: When parents raise children according to a paradigm other than the biblical paradigm, they will have an increase of problems; they will become exasperated, and they will exasperate their children. All of this exasperation is avoided, Paul said, if one brings up one's children "in the training and instruction of the Lord."

As Paul was Jesus's disciple, so a child is to be his or her parents' disciple. The exasperation of which Paul spoke prevents discipleship. Instead of causing a child to want to listen, it causes the child to want to be somewhere else. Instead of bringing about good behavior, its inherent inconsistency brings about a confusion of behavior, good and bad. Instead of causing a child to look up with respect and admiration, exasperation causes the child to regard the parent as, at best, a servant who is there to indulge and, at worst, an annoyance.

Is it pie-in-the-sky to think that parenthood can be exasperation free? Paul obviously didn't think so. And note, Paul did not say, "Now, I know some children are more vexing than others," or, "Except for those fathers whose children have attention deficit disorder, for my sympathies lie with them." He said, clearly, that if you, a parent, are exasperated with (and therefore exasperating to) your children, you are not bringing them up in a manner consistent with God's design. Paul was intimately familiar with God's Word. He knew that Scripture (Paul's Scripture, remember, was what we today call the Old Testament) is chock-full of child-rearing wisdom.

Didn't Work, Isn't Working, Won't Work

It's worth repeating: Postmodern Psychological Parenting has not worked, is not working, and never will work. It was failed from the get-go, a flop before it got off the ground. Because it represents a radical departure from the child-rearing plan set forth in the Bible, any attempt to get PPP to work will fail—it will exasperate all concerned.

Because PPP is a cobbled-together hodgepodge of Freudian, humanistic, and behavioral theory, it cannot serve as a coherent guide for parents. Furthermore, because of the many competing opinions constantly issuing forth from the Tower of Parent-Babble, it is impossible for parents who subscribe (whether wittingly or not) to PPP to be consistent, on one track, about anything. Confusion does not lend itself to consistency. Confusion breeds confusion, and confusion breeds exasperation.

God's Word: Consistent and Coherent

A coherent, never-changing point of view is prerequisite to consistent parenting. The only coherent, never-changing point of view concerning children is provided in Scripture. If you want to be consistent in your parenting, you had better subscribe to God's Word; it's as simple as that.

The Bible's parenting plan does not prescribe specific parenting behavior; it does not stipulate specific "how-tos" as in how to deal with sibling rivalry or how to correct a misbehaving child in a store. Rather, it describes the proper point of view that parents should acquire and to which they should adhere.

Parents who acquire that proper point of view will know what to do about siblings who bicker and a child who misbehaves in a store and all the other problems that can arise in the course of raising children. Today's parents have no clear point of view, so they rely on methods and strategies like time-out and 1-2-3 Magic[4] and star charts and the like. In so doing, they put the cart before the horse and condemn themselves to inconsistency and themselves and their children to exasperation.

It is indeed important that your approach to parenting issues be consistent from day to day, but as you will soon discover, your actual disciplinary *tactics* can vary from day to day without compromising the consistency of your general *approach* to discipline.

To be consistent in your approach, however, you must be consistent in your attitude—the way you carry yourself. In all situations, at all times, your composure and your authority should shine through. Composure is a function of being supremely confident that you are doing the right thing. (And keep in mind that doing the right thing doesn't mean you have to do the very best thing that you could have done. Doing the right thing doesn't mean being perfect.) In your role as parent, you should *always* carry yourself with calm, purposeful, authoritative confidence. The consistency of your attitude *confirms* your values, your vision, and your determination to stay the course on your child's behalf under any and all circumstances, all of which should be reflected in *everything* you do and *everything* you say to your child. Look here! It says so in Deuteronomy, in the very first of God's instructions to parents! "These commandments that I give you today are to be upon your hearts. Impress them on your children. Talk about them when you sit at home and when you walk along the road, when you lie down and when you get up" (Deuteronomy 6:6–7).

You cannot be supremely confident you are doing the right thing unless you are supremely confident in the source that informs your point of view, and I am bold enough to say that the

Bible is the *only* source that can possibly inspire that confidence and composure.

Consistent, but Not Predictable

Consistent behavior confirms a parent's purpose, vision, and determination. By being consistent, a parent demonstrates that nothing her child does will knock her off course. Her child-rearing "aim" never wavers from the direction in which she wants her child "to go" (Proverbs 22:6, also Chapter 7 of this book). When today's parents think of consistency, they think in terms that reflect the influence of the reigning behavior modification model: To wit, every time a child misbehaves in some specific manner, parents should respond with the same old, same old consequence.

For example, every time an eight-year-old refuses to do what one of his parents tells him to do, the parent should make him sit in the time-out chair for fifteen minutes. That's consistent, all right, but children "immunize" fairly quickly to consequences they learn to predict. It isn't going too take many trips to the time-out chair for said six-year-old to regard time-out as just a minor inconvenience.

In addition, the eventual realization that his parents are more bothered by his defiance than he is by time-out may cause him to defy them that much more! In the final analysis, then, this sort of consistency—consistency of method, especially when the method isn't that discomforting in the first place—can turn bad behavior into horrifying behavior.

Indeed, parents should make every effort to deliver consequences consistently, but one can be consistent in that regard without being predictable. For example, the next time our rebellious eight-year-old defies his parents, I'd encourage them to put him in the time-out chair for an hour! Upon his next act of insubordination, I'd have them send him to his room until he has written, neatly, "I will obey my parents because they love me" one hundred times. The next incident could result in his parents' taking his bicycle away for a month. And so on. This approach to the delivery of consequences prevents immunization and keeps the child "on his toes" (or, "minding his ps and qs"[5]) because he cannot predict what's going to happen when he misbehaves.

From the Garden to the Briar Patch

A parent asks, "So how far can you take this? What if this child's parents do all of that and he keeps right on defying them? How far can his parents go with consequences before they run out of options?"

At some point, I'd have the parents kick His Most Royal Rebelliousness out of the "Garden of Eden." Said eight-year-old comes home from school one day to find that every belonging save essential furniture and essential clothing has been removed from his room (and put into a storage locker some distance from the home). Any possessions elsewhere in the house, including the garage, have been likewise removed and stored. His Garden of Eden has become a briar patch! His parents calmly inform him that over the next month he must obey every single instruction they give him and every single rule they have ever described to him before he will begin getting his possessions back, but even then, he will only get one possession back per "perfect" day, beginning with his least-favorite thing. Furthermore, if he is twenty days into the month and incurs an infraction, his penitential month will begin over again the next day. Furthermore, if and when he manages to begin getting his booty back and commits an infraction, everything he has earned back will be taken away and he will have to start over again. I call it "kicking the child out of the garden" for obvious reasons. That seemed to have a profoundly memorable effect on the human race, after all.

> *So the LORD God banished them from the Garden of Eden, and he sent Adam out to cultivate the ground from which he had been made.*
>
> —*GENESIS 3:23 (NLT)*

Someone might argue, "But that didn't cure human rebelliousness! What if being kicked out of the 'garden' doesn't cure a child's rebelliousness either? What do you do then?"

The same thing God has done: hang in there. Twice in Jeremiah, God laments that nothing he has done has succeeded at causing his chosen people to listen to and obey him. "Yet they did not listen or pay attention; they were stiff-necked and would not listen or respond to discipline" (Jeremiah 17:23). "They turned their backs to me and not their faces; though I taught them again and again, they would not listen or respond to discipline" (Jeremiah 32:33).

If God has this continuing problem with his children, there will definitely be times when you have the same problem. Therefore, the Jeremiah Principle: *If a child does a wrong thing, and his parents do the right thing, there is no guarantee the child will begin doing the right thing.* If you run up against the Jeremiah Principle with one of your children, you should keep right on doing the right thing and pray for him—a lot.

I've known of children who were kicked out of the garden and kept right on doing their rebellious thing for months thereafter. Acting impervious to consequences is nothing more than another form of rebellion, after all. Most of these kids eventually came around. But not all of them did, and that is just the way things sometimes turn out when you're dealing with human beings.

A parent, somewhere: "So what should I do if they never come around?"

John: "You should do as little for them as the law will allow, and you should love them as much as your heart will allow, and you should emancipate them as soon as possible, and you should let the real world become their teacher, and you should keep on praying."

It's a bit difficult, I admit, to come up with creative consequences when the pressure is on. To deal with that, I've had parents write ten consequences on ten small pieces of paper, which they then fold and put in a goldfish bowl. When the child misbehaves, the parents draw from the bowl. Whatever is written on the paper they drew is the child's punishment. This somewhat playful approach is validated by two findings: First, children do not like it (which might suffice); second, misbehavior drops drastically in both frequency and strength.

The Referee's Rule

When it comes to how you handle misbehavior, the most important of all considerations is what I call the Referee's Rule: no threats, second chances, or deals. If instead of simply calling fouls when they occurred and assessing the proper penalties, a basketball referee threatened ("If you do that one more time, I'll have to blow the whistle on you!"), gave second chances ("How many times do I have to tell you not to run into a player while he's got the ball!"), or made deals ("I'll overlook that if you promise to wash my car when the game's over") when fouls were committed, the game would quickly deteriorate into chaos. Likewise, when a parent threatens, cajoles, and so forth when his or her children misbehave, chaos will reign in the home. Whenever a parent tells me that his kids are driving him crazy, I know I'm talking to a parent who does nothing consistently except violate the Referee's Rule, all the while becoming more and more exasperated. Finally, said parent explodes, thus transferring his exasperation to his children. For a while, things are relatively calm, but it's not long before the level of chaos begins its upward creep all over again, to the tune of threats, second chances, and deals. This parent is his own worst enemy. The problem is his management of his children, not that they were born to be forever wild.

Questions for Group Discussion or Personal Reflection

1. Do your children know that your word can be relied upon, that it is the law? Does each of them know, beyond a shadow of doubt, that when you say yes you mean nothing short of yes? Do they know that when you say no you mean no? If not, why not? Are you willing to accept full responsibility for the problem?

2. When you give instructions to your children, do you demand or command? Do you use leadership speech or are you guilty of using Milquetoast speech? If the latter, did your parents talk in that fashion to you? If not, what has caused you to do with your children what your parents did not do with you?

3. If you were the parent whose child threw his belongings all over the house after school, would you have been incredulous at John's recommendation? Is it difficult for you to lower the boom on your children when they misbehave? Do you find yourself dealing with the same issues over and over and over again? If so, are you willing to accept that your reluctance to cause your children prolonged discomfort when they misbehave is a major part of the problem?

4. Can you think of a recent occasion when lowering the boom would have been appropriate? How could you have done so? What do you think would be different today if you had?

5. Can you think of a recent occasion when you punished ineffectually because you thought you had to punish right away? What would you have done differently if you had known then that it was okay to delay the delivery of the consequence?

6. How would your parenting be different today if you'd read this book five years ago?

7. A thought problem: Your ten-year-old talks back to his teacher. What could you do to minimize the likelihood that he will ever again talk back to a teacher?

8. A thought problem: You find an empty beer can under the driver's seat of your sixteen-year-old son's car. He swears he doesn't know how it got there. What do you do?

9. A thought problem: Your four-year-old is disruptive in his preschool class. His teacher suggests that he might have attention deficit disorder. What could you do to cure his disorder, to set his brain chemicals back in balance?

AFTERWORD

Journalists often ask me if I think the overall parenting situation in America is getting worse or better. I see signs of both, actually.

On the one hand, every year, teachers tell me classroom behavior is more of a problem than it was the year before, also that the behavioral problems themselves are becoming more outrageous. The recent surge in home-schooling began with Christian parents but now includes many secular parents who are concerned about the quality of education their children receive and the social influences they're exposed to in public school. Pediatricians spend more time counseling parents concerning behavioral issues than treating sick children. The mental health of America's kids keeps deteriorating. I don't think we've hit bottom yet.

On the other hand, more and more parents are realizing that Postmodern Psychological Parenting has been a complete failure and are embracing or wanting to embrace the traditional, biblical model. Ten years ago, it was not unusual for people to storm out of my talks or even to shout at me from the floor. I've experienced nothing of that sort in quite some time. Increasingly, people who are not Christians come to my biblically based presentations and seminars, wanting to understand the foundations of traditional child rearing.

I can come up with only one explanation for these two simultaneous trends: American parenting is becoming bipolar. When the chips stop falling, one camp will consist of parents who stubbornly adhere to the psychological, self-esteem-based paradigm; who will deny that the ship is sinking until the water is over the gunwales, or longer. The other will be made up of a growing number of parents who adopt the traditional, biblical model. Some of these parents are looking for any alternative to the psychological model, but I'm sure God is no less involved in their recovery than he is for Christian parents who have wandered like the prodigal and are now coming back home.

I am definitely concerned about the future of America. Functional child rearing strengthens culture, and dysfunctional child rearing weakens it. Postmodern Psychological Parenting has weakened America, perhaps irreparably. For the past few years, I have been advising parents to do all they can to isolate their children from popular culture. If you feel up to it, I say, educate your children in your home, where you can control the curriculum as well as their exposure to peers. Eliminate television from your children's lives until they are fully literate, and from that point use it as an educational tool, but with great discretion. Don't let your children, even teens, on the Internet without your supervision. Be a cultural and media filter in your children's lives, and as were librarians in a bygone era, be ruthless in that regard. The Serpent is alive and well, and as always he is intent upon getting your children's attention so he can "broaden their knowledge."

My immediate concern has to do with the fact that nearly two generations of children have been raised according to psychobabble. They call themselves things like Generation X. I call them Generation E, for entitlement. They cannot distinguish between what they want and what they truly need, so they consume indiscriminately, everything from food to entertainment. They have little tolerance for frustration or ability to delay gratification, so they lack frugality. What they want, they think they deserve to have. They believe they deserve problem-free marriages, so they will not be married long if at all, assuming the institution even survives the deconstructionist onslaught. They believe obligation is a one-way street that flows in their direction, so they will not be good neighbors, employees, or citizens. My description does not apply to every single child of the entitlement generation, but it applies to too many. More than anything I am concerned that few among today's young people will sacrifice for any good greater than themselves, and not for long at that. I am concerned that they will grow up and look to government to provide the same entitlements their parents provided, the same free ride. But I am most concerned that few of today's young people will be willing to take up arms to defend freedom when and wherever it is threatened.

As I was finishing this book, a journalist called me to ask what I thought about the new parenting rage in her community: programs that give toddlers the "right start" in learning yoga, a musical instrument, gymnastics, ballet, and soccer, to name but a handful. I thought immediately of a song by Sonny and Cher: "The Beat Goes On." This sort of foolishness is emblematic of Postmodern Psychological Parenting. Like my parents and their peers, today's parents want their children to succeed. Unlike my parents and most of their peers, many of today's parents obviously think of success in largely material terms. They think success is playing Carnegie Hall at the age of six, being invited to dance with the American Ballet Company at the age of eight, or winning a soccer scholarship to Stanford. They don't seem to understand or want to accept that in the final analysis, success is about character; that an honest man who sweeps the floor of a major corporation is more successful in the real sense than the dishonest man who is its CEO. But these parents seek not just material and social success for their children, but success for themselves. In today's parenting world, honor goes to the parents who raise the trophy child who plays Carnegie Hall at age six, and so on. There is no bumper sticker that reads "My Child Has Impeccable Manners!"

In the short term, I'm pessimistic. I don't think the overall parenting situation in America is going to get any better, not any time soon at least. We lives in times of trouble and tribulation made all the worse by the fact that there is no consensus concerning how children should be raised, much less things even more fundamental, like the definitions of marriage and family. A culture that lacks such consensus is a culture at the edge of the abyss. In the long term, however, I'm optimistic. Things are going to get worse before they get better, but I'm confident they will get better. The Bible tells me so.

America needs more than anything else a retro-parenting revolution. The bad news is that the revolution isn't coming any time soon. America's parenting problems are too grave, and too many parents are too deeply into denial. The good news is that any parents who so choose can bring about a parenting revolution in their homes, beginning today.

How about you? You can put down this book and resolve that things will never again be the same in your household.

Go ahead. Do it. Everybody's counting on you, whether they know it or not.

HOW TO USE THIS BOOK

This book can be used to structure a six- to twelve-week parenting program. If six weeks, I suggest that instead of trying to discuss all eleven chapters plus Introduction and Afterword, each class session begin with one thirty-minute DVD from the accompanying series (see below), and that only Chapters 5 through 11 be discussed in class, using the questions found at the end of each chapter. If eight weeks, Part One can be added to the discussion schedule by discussing Chapters 1 and 2 in the first session and Chapters 2 and 3 in the second session. At that point, pick up on the six-week program described above. If the discussion program is twelve weeks in length, I recommend devoting one class session to Chapters 1 and 2, one session to Chapters 3 and 4, and then one session each to Chapters 5 through 8. Chapters 10 and 11 should each be given two sessions. In any case, Chapter 9 should be left for individual reading and contemplation.

For those reading the book on their own, I recommend that married couples read it together and likewise use the questions at the end of each chapter to guide life-changing discussion. It is my most sincere hope, by the way, that the lives of those who read this book are changed irrevocably and for the much, much better. I recommend that any single parent who reads this book should first find another single parent "partner" with whom to share the experience and the responsibility for keeping each other on track—a mini support group, if you will. The more the merrier and more meaningful is my belief, so I strongly encourage couples and singles to form, on their own, discussion groups. I also encourage parents who attend church- or school-based discussion groups and parents who form independent discussion groups to continue meeting on a regular basis after the "coursework" is finished to provide continuing support and sustenance to one another. Be a church!

This book is supplemented by a DVD series that features the author speaking, in his typically provocative and humorous style, to an audience gathered in a church. The DVD series is intended for use by church groups that have formed for the purpose of reading and discussing *Parenting by The Book*. A CD series, great for listening to in one's car, is also available. For ordering information, email Willie at willie@rosemond.com and reference "PBTB DVD series," or order directly from www.parentingbythebook.com. Both series will be updated and supplemented by CDs and DVDs on a regular basis, and any group or individual ordering either series will receive notification of the latest updates and be informed of future updates.

NOTES

Chapter 1: *The Walls Come Crumblin' Down*

1. The biblical child-rearing paradigm was so thoroughly embedded in American culture that even people who were not believers in any way, shape, or form raised their children according to biblical principles, however unwittingly.

2. Gordon, Thomas. *Teaching Children Self-Discipline* (New York: Times Books Random House, 1989), 239.

3. *Your Child's Self-Esteem* (New York: Doubleday, 1970).

4. Relatively recent scientific discoveries have all but proven false the notion popularized by astronomer Carl Sagan (1924–98) that life-sustaining planets abound in the universe. Objective evidence to the effect that Earth is the one and only such planet, and that there has never been and will never be another such planet, is growing stronger every day.

Chapter 2: *Postmodern Psychological Parenting*

1. *Newsweek,* March 16, 2006.

2. See Exodus 3:6. The child's assertion that he is God, that his authority is first and final, is the root of all sin.

3. *Chronicles* magazine, December 2006.

4. From the National Center for Health Statistics publication *Death Rates for 72 Selected Causes, by 5-year Age Groups, Race, and Sex: United States, 1979–95,* available on line at http://www.cdc.gov/nchswww/data/gm291_1.pdf.

Chapter 3: The Serpent's Currency

1. By using the word "seduced" I mean to make clear that today's parents have every reason to think that doing everything they can to ensure high self-esteem is what good parenting is all about. My wife and I fell for PPP and were held in its seductive sway for the first nine of our parenthood years. I am, therefore, all too familiar with the corrosive effect it has on the family. American parents need to liberate themselves from the new paradigm, and I believe that only the *real, honest-to-goodness* truth as found in the Bible can make that happen. Before one can release oneself from a prison, however, one must know its "layout." That's my purpose in this and the previous chapter: I'm describing the prison of PPP—what it looks and feels like—so that parents can find their way out.

2. "Helicopter Parents Hit the Job Market" (AP November 7, 2006). (This article is no longer available online, but for a secondary reference, see Bob Goldman, "Work Daze," http://funnybusiness.com/2006_03_01_archive.html.)

Chapter 4: The Tower of Parent-Babble

1. Protagoras (c 481–c 411 B.C.), a Greek philosopher sometimes called the first humanist because he put man at the center of knowledge.

2. *Parent Effectiveness Training* (Wyden, 1970), 27.

3. Ibid, 213.

4. Many people in the secular world associate the Bible with guilt. But whereas some religious denominations promote false doctrines that cause guilt in their followers, the Bible is not a source of guilt. Quite the contrary, the Bible is a source of comfort, of promise, of salvation from guilt. In postmodern America, the new secular religion of psychology is the primary source of guilt. As Grandma used to say, "Doesn't that beat all?!"

Chapter 5: Parenting as One Flesh

1. This description may seem silly to or even offend the sensibilities of "modern" women who view such traditional wifely behavior as submissively demeaning, but I propose that this describes submission to God's instructions, not submission to males. Keep in mind also that the husband in this description is submitting to God's instructions as well. He is not coming home to play with his children or sit in front of the television set watching sports; he is coming home with one purpose in mind: to be with his wife.

2. A paradoxical title, given that the book is actually a guide for having a wonderful relationship with one's kids.

Chapter 6: Character First

1. A story for anyone who thinks that video games are not actually addictive: In September 2006, Willie and I stayed at a hotel in San Francisco that had recently hosted a "gamers" convention. The hotel staff told me that the participants were so wrapped up in playing their games that they forgot to drink water. Several had become dehydrated. To avoid lawsuits, the hotel staff had to give the participants bottled water and insist that they drink. If that does not describe addictive behavior, I don't know what does!

2. Susan Reusberger, *The Complete Idiot's Guide to Understanding the Amish* (New York: Alpha, 2003), 15.

Chapter 10: Leadership Discipline

1. I acknowledge, by the way, that behavior modification works fairly well with children with pronounced developmental problems. It also appears to work in tightly controlled institutional settings, but selectively, and "appears" is the operative word.

2. Thomas Sowell, www.jewishworldreview.com.

Chapter 11: Command, Compel, Confirm

1. Caspar Milquetoast was created by Harold Webster in 1924 for his comic strip *The Timid Soul,* from which "milquetoast" has come to mean "weak and ineffectual." Webster continued to produce the strip until his death in 1952. The name is a deliberate misspelling of a bland and rather inoffensive food, milk toast (http://en.wikipedia.org/wiki/Caspar_Milquetoast).

2. There is debate over the origin of this expression, but *The American Heritage Dictionary of Idioms* (1997) says it refers to the boom of a sailboat, a long spar that extends from the mast to hold the foot of the sail. In a changing wind, the boom can swing wildly, leaving one at risk of being struck.

3. Diana Baumrind, University of California Berkeley.

4. For more information, see www.parentmagic.com.

5. The most convincing explanation of this delightful idiom is that it comes from the early days of printing, when movable type had to be positioned upside-down. The lowercase letters p and q were difficult to distinguish since they are mirror images. "Mind your ps and qs" was occasionally shouted out to remind everyone to . . . mind their ps and qs. It eventually came to mean being on one's best behavior.

ABOUT THE AUTHOR

When John graduated from graduate school in 1972, he and Willie had one child, Eric. Shortly thereafter, daughter Amy came along. At the time, they were learning, and have continued to learn, their lessons the hard way. Then they became grandparents, which has been nothing but easy. They subscribe to the adage, first coined by John (or so he claims) that it is the grandparents' job to spoil a child and the parents' job to see to it that the child never becomes spoiled. They now have six grandchildren and one on the way due in September 2007.

Since graduation, John has directed child mental health programs, spent eleven or so years in private practice, written eleven books on raising children, and, since 1976, written a nationally syndicated parenting column that now appears weekly in more than 250 newspapers across the United States, including Alaska, Hawaii, and St. Thomas, U.S. Virgin Islands.

Eight months out of the year, John is on the road, mostly speaking on parenting and family matters to parent and professional audiences nationwide. He's also spoken in London, Brussels, Barcelona, Istanbul, Guadalajara, San Juan, St. Thomas, and various locales in Canada. He gives some two hundred presentations a year, which is why he takes four months away from the road to spend with Willie, doing as close to nothing as they can possibly do. To arrange for John to speak to your community, school, church, or professional organization, contact Willie Rosemond at 704-864-1012 or WHrosemond@aol.com.

John's two primary websites are at www.rosemond.com and www.parentingbythebook.com, the former being his general site and the latter being the site that reflects his ministry to parents.